Shepherd's Warning

Shepherd's Warning

ELIZABETH GOWANS

Hamish Hamilton · London

To Anne and to Ellen

First published in Great Britain 1985 by
Hamish Hamilton Children's Books
Garden House   57–59 Long Acre   London WC2E 9JZ
Copyright © 1985 by Elizabeth Gowans
All Rights Reserved

British Library Cataloguing in Publication Data
Gowans, Elizabeth
Shepherd's warning
I. Title
823'914   [J]   PZ7
ISBN 0-241-11569-8

Typeset by Katerprint Co. Ltd, Oxford
Printed in Great Britain by
Thetford Press Ltd., Thetford, Norfolk

Contents

1	Storm Born	1
2	Killer and Stray	15
3	Signs of an Unknown Enemy	31
4	Sheep's Clothing	37
5	Stravaiging away from Troubles	49
6	Night Boat to Morlie Bay	62
7	Behind the Old Door	83
8	A Long Day Learning	92
9	Pet Days	105
10	Death in the Haggs	118
11	Something for Nosey Folk	127
12	The Game's a Bogey	145
13	The High Danger Pipe	154
14	The Sad Baddie	163
15	Tokens of a Bonny Day	170

"A red sky at night is a shepherd's delight,
A red sky in the morning is a shepherd's warning."

"The ev'ning red and the morning grey,
Are tokens of a bonny day."

Old Sayings

1

Storm Born

About a mile inland from the sea, beyond the green coastal fields where the heather moor began, the children of Ewan Blair, shepherd at Mowdy Mains, discovered a ship one blustery March morning.

It had been a night of gale force winds and driving rain, not unusual for that part of western Scotland at that time of year. The Blairs knew that all the burns around the farm would be up, maybe a few big trees would be down, and so they were off to look at the floods and the fallen.

Rannie and Jocky, the quick ones, aged nine and seven, were the first out of the door, still tugging on their wellingtons.

"Ballin Burn'll be well up!"

"It'll be a great flood!"

"Trees'll be washed away!"

"And bits of bank!"

Zipping up their anoraks as they ran, they made for Ballin Glen where the biggest burn flowed and was, therefore, likely to be the most spectacular. Behind them, coated, booted and scarved, almost stiff with wrappings against the wind, laboured five-year-old Nan, desperate not to miss the sights.

"Rannie. Wait for me! I want to see the flood, too!"

Eleven-year-old Gardner, in a long oilskin coat and his grandfather Blair's old knitted balaclava, loped along after the others, just as eager to see the effects of the storm but also mindful of the younger ones perhaps getting too close to rushing water. Rannie especially was prone to sudden accident wherever he walked the earth!

"Rannie!" Gardner called. "Watch where you're going. Ca' canny! Wait for the rest of us, now!"

Betsy, the eldest child at twelve, followed rather more slowly in the rear. She'd recently been ill and wasn't quite up to battling with the elements yet, although their mother said a walk in the fresh air was just what she needed now. Betsy got as far as the first gate when she realised what she needed was an extra jumper under her coat in this wind. She turned back to fetch one from the porch.

Their parents were talking in low voices in the kitchen. Betsy heard the words that passed between them and the troubled tones in which they spoke. She quietly got the jumper on and her coat re-buttoned. Then she set off to catch up with the others, her mind flooded with concern for them all, her heart sore at the prospect of such a change in their lives. How could she tell the others? Obviously, since their parents had waited till they were alone to discuss the matter, the Blair children weren't supposed to know. That meant, Betsy lamented to herself, *she'd* have to keep her own counsel. She picked her way through the boggy bits of the hill, following well-known safe routes, and came at last to where the others were gathered, gazing and pointing at the first spectacle produced by the storm.

A whole line of beeches lay on the ground, some with their roots torn up and splayed in the air, others snapped off in mid-trunk. They'd grown on a particularly exposed part of the moor forming part of an old field. The Blairs had swung and climbed in them on many a day.

"Seven of them!" exclaimed Rannie. He was awe-struck at the sight, for it was shocking to see things they'd trusted to hold them safely now so broken. For Betsy, at that moment, the sight of them added to her sense of dismay at what she already knew.

"Let's go and see the burn!" cried Rannie. "Bet it's over its banks!"

"Aye, it will be," warned Gardner, grabbing his brother's arm. "You better watch *you* don't go over its banks the *other* way! Mind, now! I don't fancy fishing you out. You might not be so lucky this time, Rannie!"

Rannie tugged away from Gardner, not liking to be reminded of the time he'd fallen into Ettrick Water as a small child and been miraculously hooked out of the torrent by the gaff that their father had been using to fish with downstream. All the same, he slowed down and stayed by the others as they made their way carefully into Ballin Glen.

They could hear the sound of rushing water long before they reached the bottom of the slope, and underneath that sound was the deeper, rumbling tone of the very deepest pools filling up. Indeed, as they came at last within sight of the flooded burn, the very earth seemed to shake with the beat of the turbulent water.

"We'll not go any nearer that bank, you lot!" Betsy announced, her arms out on either side to hold them back. "It could be ready to wash away any minute. This is near enough."

She hardly needed to caution them, for they all felt, despite the fascination of the torrent, an instinctive holding back. Still, Rannie for one wanted somehow to test the swiftness of the water. He picked up a twig and cast it into the stream where it immediately sped out of sight and was lost over the first boulder.

"Get something bigger," suggested Jocky. "Here! This branch'll do."

The two of them heaved the fallen branch once, twice, and on the third swing let it fly across the intervening space. It made a satisfying, splendid splash, went under, and resurfaced, forging downstream on the current. They watched it up-end itself over boulders, settle down to smoother sailing beyond them, and finally it too was lost to sight round the bend.

"That was a good one. C'mon, we'll do it again."

Three more were launched, the last being a thing

almost too heavy for them, even with Betsy and Gardner helping. This forked branch rode high in the water, one fork sticking up with twig-tips trembling.

"Look!" said Wee Nan. "It's like a ship."

"Yes," breathed Rannie, seeing it with her eyes. "You could sit on one of them and it'd carry you down all the road to the sea. What d'you bet it would?"

"Maybe aye, and maybe hooch aye," said Gardner, using their family's time-honoured reply for discouraging fanciful thoughts. "C'mon, we'll follow it up the way and see what's what, eh?"

He looked at Betsy who was still staring at the water but not really seeing it. "What's wrong with *you*?"

She started. "Nothing. C'mon, Nan, take my hand."

They began to follow the well-known burn upstream, still marvelling at the different aspects of the flood round each familiar bend. Strange waterfalls and cataracts had appeared, carrying broken branches and torn clumps of rushes. Then came the long, smooth, rather sinister curving stretch where the water always seemed to flow more slowly, so that the eye, too, slowed and dwelt on it. They all saw the leaning tree and the floating object ahead.

"It's a sheep, Gardner," Betsy called out. "She's alive! She must have just fallen in."

"She's going to be swept away, unless . . . !"

Gardner cast about for some way to help the stricken animal struggling in the water, her fleece getting heavier every second, pulling her under.

With a speed that he only rarely summoned — what the rest of them called Gardner's "mad cow dash", referring to the time he'd leapt amazingly fast out of the path of a hurtling mad cow — Gardner was into the tree leaning low over the water and had reached down to grasp in the nick of time the small horn of the sheep as she passed beneath. Rannie followed suit instantly, grasping the other horn, and, between the two of them, they managed to guide the animal to a little natural bay made by the tree's exposed roots in the bank. From there they hauled the dripping sheep to safety. She staggered for a moment on her feet, then began to run away, shaking herself. At a safe distance, she turned to look at her rescuers and gave herself another shake before moving slowly off up the wooded slope, already bent on grazing.

Gardner and Rannie inched off the leaning tree, looking after the sheep.

"Quick work there!" Jocky said admiringly. "She'd have drowned if you hadn't grabbed her."

"She might not have, if she hadn't been in lamb," replied Gardner, sucking at a torn knuckle.

"So we've really saved *two* sheep!" exulted Rannie. "Wait till we tell Dad *that*."

Mention of their father reminded Betsy of her secret knowledge and her spirits, momentarily lifted by the rescue, fell again. She wanted to share her sadness with the others very badly.

"That's *another* ship," Wee Nan was saying out loud to herself. The others turned from watching the departing ewe. Wee Nan was looking at the tree from which the rescue had been performed. Now they looked with her, recognising it despite its altered position.

The tree had once been a fairly unremarkable though ancient beech growing by the burn. Last night's violent gale and flood had transformed it. The force of the wind had tilted the huge giant over the water. The torrent of the swollen burn had washed away the earth up to and around the great roots, forming a wide pool. One large, twisting nether branch swept out low over the water now in a wonderful, prow-like curve. When Gardner and Rannie had used it to reach the ewe, nobody had had eyes for anything else but the rescue. But now! Now they could see what Wee Nan meant by a ship.

Very carefully, they tried it out. There were plenty of hand-holds, plenty of foot-holds, plenty of forks in which to sit, near the water yet safe from it. Wee Nan could even come on board, courtesy of a special network of roots at the base.

"Hey! I can make it move!" Rannie called. "Here's what you do. You have to stare at the water *and* the edge of a branch. See? It feels like moving along. Ahoy, there, shipmates!"

Jocky leaned over, following Rannie's instructions. After a moment he made a retching noise. "Makes me seasick!" he said, looking truly nauseated before grinning.

Betsy knew that feeling, from the very first bridge she'd ever crossed, a swing-bridge over the fateful Ettrick Water. That, too, had been a flood-time and she'd crossed the bridge, clutching their father's hand, on her first day of school.

"This is a great place!" Jocky said. "I like this place where we live now. Hands up who likes Mowdy Mains, eh?" He was excited by the discovery of the ship, by the flood sounds all around.

"Yes," Gardner was saying, "this is one of the best places we've ever lived, I suppose." Betsy listened to him with fresh dismay. "And when you think of all the things that happened just last year, it makes you feel you've maybe *earned* the place, sort of."

"That's right," Rannie agreed. "We've staked our claim. That's what you call it. We've named bits of this place, saved it from rustlers —"

"— put out a terrible heather fire," added Jocky.

"And don't forget Jack," said Gardner quietly. "We've helped Jack."

"Good old Tattie Bogle!" Rannie cheered, shaking himself on his rigging, so that the whole ship shook. "Whoops! Steady as she goes!"

Betsy thought of Jack Tattersall, their friend, a solitary Yorkshire boy and fellow-stravaiger, who had chosen them to befriend him long before they knew of his existence and who had allowed himself to be found by them later when he had "dispeared" from the tree-house in which he'd lived alone.

"And," Betsy said, remembering their other, much older friend who'd also been solitary until Jack took refuge with her and they'd adopted each other, "thanks to us, nobody calls Flo Jinty a witch any more."

They were silent for a while, watching the water, enjoying the tree-ship and their sense of belonging. It was Wee Nan who shattered the moment.

"Betsy? When is the November term?"

"In November — in eight months' time. Why?"

Wee Nan sighed. "Well, that's when we'll have to leave here."

They stared at her, puzzled — all except Betsy who was astonished and relieved that now she could speak.

"What's she havering about?" snorted Rannie, shaking the ship again.

"I'm *not* havering," Wee Nan protested. "I heard Daddie saying it."

"When?"

"I can't remember. But I heard. I was sleeping in Mummy's lap, only I wasn't sleeping."

"Well, there you are," said Gardner, "you were dreaming it."

"No. She wasn't." Betsy went to her sister and sat among the roots with her. "She heard right. *I* heard them talking today when I went back for a jersey.

They were talking about us leaving here all right."

Gardner looked at her sharply. "Why?"

"I don't know. But I do know they don't want to. Dad said something like us being *forced* to go. I wish I knew what the trouble is, but they don't want us to know, it seems."

"Well," Gardner murmured, "in that case, we'd better not let on that we *do*."

Everybody nodded glumly. "Still," Betsy offered, "maybe the next place we go to, wherever it is, will be another fine bit. We've always managed after other flittings, even when Mum didn't like the new place."

"But I don't *want* to leave here! Not for *ages*! It's like . . . like having to go home before you've finished the game," Rannie cried angrily.

"Aye, so it is!" agreed Jocky. "Or like clearing the table before a laddie's had one of everything that's there. No very fair!"

"Well, it's eight months away still. We'll just have to make the most of the time that's left, that's all," reasoned Gardner.

"*I* know!" Rannie exclaimed. "When the lorry comes for us, we could all hide and then go and live with Tattie Bogle. I've always wanted to wangle some way to stay in that tree-house. Anyway, that's what *I'm* going to do when the time comes."

The others allowed him to comfort himself with this decision, without a word of mockery or reproach for such a plan, one that would surely trouble their mother in the best Rannie tradition. After all, they had eight months to think up some way to curb him!

They were all gazing at the water moving strongly past beneath them. Betsy thought of the saying about a lot of water flowing under the bridge. It usually had something to do with events gone by that didn't matter any more, they had happened so long ago. Right enough, maybe if you watched water flowing by like this for long enough, all sorts of things might stop mattering so much. She tried it letting her eyes glaze over.

Suddenly, a violent cracking and a splash disturbed the water just out of her circle of vision. She immediately thought it was Rannie incapable of proceeding any further with his day in total safety. But he was there, still in the ship's "rigging" above her.

"Who threw that?" he shouted, as startled as she was. They were all alert, disturbed at the sudden noise, all eyes on the water.

They looked around at the trees lining the banks on either side of the burn and then, with one accord, as the answer dawned on them, they gave a cheer. Rannie rocked in his rigging, Gardner swished the water with a twig, Jocky thumped the branch above him, while Betsy and Nan scrambled to their feet in welcome.

"Come aboard, Tattie Bogle!"
"How d'you like our ship?"
"Come and be a tar, Jack!"

From behind a thick beech trunk a few trees upstream stepped Jack, scarved and sweatered in Flo Jinty's best knits. He gave a laugh and soon joined them "on board". "What're you calling her, then?" he asked, looking her over. "Have to have a name. *The Jolly Beech*? No. Have to do better than that."

"*The Drunken Sailor*? Get it?" suggested Rannie, at which Jocky was the first to laugh.

"No. That's too disrespectful," said Betsy. "Very punny-funny, but you have to show respect for the ship that carries you, you know. All great ships have noble names, I think."

"I've heard of one called *The Saucy Nancy*," said Jack, "which isn't very noble, but *it* was a boat. I suppose boats aren't as stately as *ships*. Anyway, don't you like found places and things to be named, on discovery, the way explorers do it? I even have names for the stones that I find."

"Oh?" Betsy was interested. "Like what?"

But he was shy about saying anything more, it seemed. Maybe another time, she thought, he'd tell them, or her.

"Anyway," she said, "she's definitely a bonnie bark, whatever she's called."

"Hey!" Jocky cried. "*The Bonnie Beech Bark*! There's your name. Bark and bark, see?" He was elated with his discovery, despite Rannie's mocking canine yelps in the twigs above. It was, Betsy decided, the best one yet, but they'd have to wait and see which name would come to mind the first

P.C. MURDOCH IS OOR WULLIE'S FRIEND

REMEMBER —THE POLICEMAN IS YOUR FRIEND

If you are ever frightened by anyone, ask a grown-up for help, or—

GO TO A POLICEMAN

The Sunday Post

OOR WULLIE'S ADVICE—

SAY 'NO' TO STRANGERS

NEVER go away with a stranger.

NEVER get into a stranger's car.

NEVER accept sweets or money from a stranger.

ALWAYS stay with your friends — and be back home before dark.

ALWAYS tell your mum or dad where you are going.

IF you are approached by a stranger tell your parents or your teacher.

IF you are ever frightened by anyone, ask a grown-up you know for help, or go to a policeman.

time they'd have need to refer to this new-found curiosity in their landscape. Only then was it that things were really and truly christened and always so remembered, even when people left them forever.

Rannie swung down to Jack's side, almost upsetting both of them into the water. "Listen, Tattie Bogle, I'm coming to live with you when the time comes for us to leave here."

Jack looked in puzzlement from one to the other of them. "You're *leaving* here? Why? When?"

Betsy explained. He put his head on the branch level with it, hiding his face. "Eight months, you're saying? Two hundred and forty something days sounds longer. And it's *thousands* of hours."

"Yes," she said, seeing how he, too, was bothered by the prospect. "A *lot* of water has to flow under the bridge — *this* bridge — before then."

Jack took out his pen-knife and, sliding down to the base of the beech, he carved a tiny, vertical stroke in the bark. "That's for the first day."

"I see," Gardner smiled at the water. "A kind of ship's *log*, eh? I wonder what sort of voyage we're going to have."

It was, Betsy thought, a good thought to have right now. It somehow helped to distance that dreaded November term and to hold out promise of at least a few worthwhile stravaigings still possible in their lives before then.

The sky above the trees had darkened, with a cold wind starting up. Drops of icy rain began to pit the surface of the water and patter on the ship's branches. The Blairs drew up their head coverings and made a hurried scramble up the slope out of the glen, leaving Jack to make an even more hurried retreat to Flo Jinty's cottage as the rain turned to hail sweeping across the Firth on the March wind.

At the top of the wooded slope, in the lea of a little bank sheltered from the blast, they passed by the rescued sheep. Newly lambed, she was licking her small offspring. As shepherds' children know to do, they did not rush over to inspect what was clearly the first lamb of the season, born perhaps a little early because of the mother's recent ordeal, but went on quietly.

"She's in a sheltered bit."

"The lamb's on its feet."

"It's sucked, as well."

"We can tell Dad where she is when we get home."

"Better run for it. Right, Nan, give us your hand."

They came down off the hill to the back door of the farm-house where their mother was looking out for them. Her look of anxiety was unmistakeable and, Betsy knew, wasn't just for their exposure to the weather.

2
Killer and Stray

That ferocious March full of red morning skies led into a sweet April, but there was no change in the troubled brow of their mother that Betsy could see — and she studied the faces of both their parents for some sign of clear weather. One Saturday, in fact, she went so far as to say, while she and their mother were outside feeding lambs, "What's wrong with you and Dad?" Their mother had looked surprised and given a little laugh.

"Och, there's nothing wrong with *us*! Don't you worry about *that*. We'll aye manage, you know, though troubles aren't scarce. Just you feed your lamb and never you mind."

Even at the best of times, this season of the year was usually fraught with uncertainty at Mowdy Mains, for it was lambing time. If the winter had been very harsh, with frost late into March, there would be little grass for the lambing ewes and their milk supply would be poor. Hungry ewes often make neglectful mothers, too. Then there was always the threat of foxes. Last spring had been a season of wonderfully sweet days but foxes had decimated fields of lambs everywhere in the countryside until three of the culprits had been hunted down and shot.

Betsy finished feeding the last lamb and looked up to the fields close to the farm. The grass didn't look bad, she thought, and there hadn't as yet been talk of foxes. She gazed beyond the fields to the moor where sheep moved slowly in a loose flock among the heather. As she watched, they suddenly began to move quickly, scattering and turning back, the movements of a flock violently disturbed. She stiffened and ran inside to fetch Gardner's old jumble-sale fieldglasses from their cleek behind the porch door. She ran back outside and trained the lenses on the bit of the hill where the sheep had been peacefully grazing minutes before. She gasped at what she saw and ran indoors.

"Mum! *Mum.* Where's Dad? There's a dog worrying sheep! It's going for them, all right! I've seen it! Out by the Blaeberry Burn."

"Oh no! Not that next!" Their mother rushed out to look. "Aye. And it's going its dinger from what I can tell. Go and find Gardner this minute. Get Jocky to run for your father."

It was one of the most dreaded situations among a hill flock and they felt the panic of it keenly. Betsy ran round to the front of the house in search of one of the boys, but they were nowhere in sight and she couldn't hear any sound of them. Even Wee Nan had disappeared. No doubt the four of them had drifted off across the fields somewhere while she was busy with the lambs. For a moment she heard herself saying, as their mother did so often, "You're *never* at home — aye stravaiging about, so you are!"

Suddenly, she did hear them. They were running urgently towards the house along the road from the direction of the lower reaches of the Blaeberry Burn. So they'd seen it too! Jocky reached her first.

"Where's Dad? We've got to get Dad!"

"I know. Is that dog still there?"

"It's no half! There'll be a *huge* massacre if it's not stopped pretty quick."

Their mother was standing at the gate with the end of her scarf up to her face, covering her mouth. "Oh Ewan, come home, man! Where *are* you?" she was saying to herself.

Gardner came panting up, distraught and unsure of what he could do. "Will I go out after it? With the gun?" he asked his mother.

"No, you'll *not*!" she said sharply. "*That* heavy thing! Leave that to your father."

"Look!" shouted Wee Nan, the sharp-eyes. "There's Daddie coming with Trim. He's running, see?"

A grim-faced Ewan Blair hurried down off the hill, his oilskins flapping, a frail, newborn lamb under his arm. Wordlessly, he gave their mother the lamb to care for while he took his gun from the Skinny Cupboard. They all watched him go, with relief and sorrow for what he would find and have to do out there on the far hill – that is, if he was in time.

Later, the Blairs having eaten, their mother having seen to the needy lamb and put it in a box by the kitchen fire, they heard their father putting his gun back in its place. He came in and sat down at the table, weary-looking. His hands were shaking, perhaps from hunger, perhaps (Betsy feared) from anger. He seemed not to see them, so preoccupied was he with some other sight and the feelings it roused in him. Their mother quietly served him with a dish of soup and, as he dipped and turned his spoon in it to cool it prior to supping, a familiar habit that often spelled thoughtfulness with him, he grew calmer.

After a few spoonfuls, he looked up and now he was seeing his children properly. They watched him eating, not wanting to ask questions with him perhaps in a black mood.

"It's the *folk* that should be shot," he muttered presently. "The way they let their damn dogs run wild. No the dogs' fault at all. But once they've tasted blood, well . . ."

"Dad?" ventured Rannie. "Did you get that one?"

Their father didn't answer right away and then he said, "I did not! He got away, all right. I never even saw the brute. Don't even know what breed he was, what size or anything. But he was big enough to tear out the throats of three fine ewes, all in lamb. I've never seen such a mess! I don't know where to start looking for the culprit, and that grates, so it does."

He stopped talking, with a helpless lift and drop of his hand.

"Dad?" Betsy began. "*I* saw that dog. Through Gardner's old fieldglasses."

He looked from her to Gardner. "You saw him? Clear-like? And what was it?"

"It was a fawny colour, with black bits, and big."

"An Alsatian?"

"I think so."

"There must be at least ten of them in the village. Still, every one of them'll need to be checked. The policeman'll be bound to tell me who all has one. Come to that, he's got one himself. Anyway, whose ever it is that did that piece of work'll be covered with blood and have sheep's wool in their belly. You're sure you saw right, now?"

Betsy was sure.

"Right. Gardner, you come with me. We'll go and see Bob Innis. We'll have to bury the dead ewes before it's dark. We'll take the spades and leave them out by till we get that other job done."

Gardner pulled on his balaclava and buttoned himself into his oilskin coat, for the skies had clouded up and rain looked to be in the offing. He and their father stepped out of the back door followed by the others who, though not included in the expedition, still put on their coats and sat on the top bar of the gate to watch their father and brother departing along the road, spades over their shoulders.

Some sheep were quietly grazing by the roadside.

Suddenly, along the road, loping easily and paying no attention to the sheep whatsoever, came a strange dog. Gardner and their father stopped in their tracks. So did the dog. A nearby ewe, bolder than most, certainly showing a moment of unusual, unsheepish bravado, advanced on the dog and stamped its forefoot sharply. The dog leaped sideways, startled, and continued its way towards the house, hesitating every few steps as it neared people.

Their father turned back to the house, gesturing to their mother at the window with a motion that suggested a gun being lifted to fire. She was to fetch his out to him quickly. *This* time, he seemed to convey from the expression on his face, the brute wouldn't get away, by Heaven!

The dog continued to advance towards them, towards its certain execution. Its coat was fawn in colour, and yet Betsy was sure this wasn't the one she'd seen among the sheep earlier. "Dad, it's not the same one!" she cried.

He glowered at her.

"C'mon wi' that gun!" he shouted through the window at their mother, ignoring Betsy's plea.

The dog approached cautiously. Their father went forward, intent on grabbing any collar there might be. As he drew near to the animal, it bared its teeth at him and growled. "Did you see that? It's a bad one all right."

Betsy knew, all of a sudden, that this was all wrong. She got down from the gate, just as their mother came out of the house empty-handed, saying, "I've been watching that dog, Ewan. That dog'd never go after sheep. The creature's feared from them. Did you see the way it shied from that ewe back there?"

Their father's voice rose in impatience. "I'm no caring! It's still up here, off the leash, among lambing ewes. I've a right to put it down. Have I no? Answer me that!"

"Aye. You have the right," she answered, low. "Nobody would deny you have the right."

"Well?" he challenged.

"Well." That one little word was all, but it seemed to say that he could go and get the gun himself if he was that keen to kill. Betsy held her breath. While their father and mother locked looks, Wee Nan went over to the dog and stroked it, fearlessly. Indeed, there was nothing to fear, for under her patting hand it was docile and pet-like. Her soft crooning voice saying "nice dog, nice dog" broke their father's desperate resolve already undermined by their mother's argument. He turned to the dog and again, as he went near, the animal growled.

He looked at their mother. "You see if it'll come to you."

She patted her knee. "Come then! Over here, lass, over here!" The dog folded its ears and came to her, wagging its tail.

The demonstration of the dog's allegiance was clear. It didn't care for men, it went willingly to a woman – and to children, for now Rannie and Jocky were stroking it without rejection.

"It's a woman's dog, all right," muttered their father. "It's got no right being up here, all the same. Damn folk! And I'm no nearer finding the one responsible for killing my sheep!"

"Oh, Ewan," murmured their mother, "meting out punishment, even if you get the right one, isn't going to help anything."

"At least I can't be said to be turning a blind eye," he retorted grimly. Listening to this exchange, Betsy felt sure it had something to do with the whole problem, whatever it was, that meant leaving Mowdy Mains.

"If you're away to see Bob Innis about the worrier, you'd better report this stray here. Maybe somebody's already missed her." Their mother fondled the dog's ears thoughtfully.

Their father shouldered his spade once more and, with a jerk of the head to Gardner, turned again towards the task ahead. Suddenly, the dog started to alert attention, ears cocked, looking to the bend in the road beyond which, hidden from view by a small beech hedge, was coming across the field the sound of voices calling.

Everyone looked in the direction of the voices and, in a moment, there came into view three figures.

The Blairs waited in silence, watchful, to see if the approaching trio was familiar. Evidently, to the dog it was abundantly so, for it left the Blairs with a joyful bound and trotted off along the road to meet the strangers who turned out to be a tall young woman accompanied by two children. They actually looked like one child twice, for they were clearly twins, perhaps a little older than Rannie. They each wore blue jeans and navy jumpers. Their short hair was the colour of thistledown. They threw themselves forward to meet the dog, calling "Janey, Janey! Where have you *been*?"

It was a classic slobbery reunion between young doting owners and lost pet. Betsy shuddered to think of the very different scene that might have taken place if their father had had his way a few minutes before. She hoped he was having similar thoughts. If he wasn't careful, she reflected, that father of theirs was going to become much too trigger-happy altogether!

The young woman stepped past the affectionate tangle of dog and twins and held out her hand to Ewan Blair. "You must be the shepherd, Mr Blair? Elenore Stewart. I'm awfully sorry about our dog going astray like this. She's a harmless old thing as far as sheep are concerned, but you couldn't know that. I know what the rules are hereabouts regarding loose dogs in lambing time and I'm terribly grateful for your forebearance. Really I am!"

Betsy watched their father's face. It was worth watching at that moment. He was always rather shy with strangers, though traditionally polite and hospitable. Now he was both shy and, if it could be said of a shepherd without mockery, rather sheepish. Then, reluctant perhaps to speak his angry thoughts to someone so nice, he turned away. Betsy could see that their mother was hiding a smile, but only for a moment, and then it was she who came out with the stern reminder, as woman to woman.

"We have just lost three ewes to a worrier out there on the hill," she said, pointing. "And then *your* dog comes stravaiging away up here. I don't know what folk were supposed to think! Anyway, it's lucky my daughter here saw the killer dog and could tell it wasn't yours."

Elenore Stewart looked suitably chagrined. "I know. Poor old Janey! She's not used to her new home yet. Nor are the twins." She looked worriedly at the two thistle-headed children now crouched by the side of the road quietly stroking their pet lying between them. "Right now they need each other badly."

She turned back to the Blairs, still waiting and watching, each filled with curiosity.

"We've just newly arrived in this part of the world, from South America. We're staying at Kilsmore Castle, with Sir Guy, your employer, I believe. He warned me that Janey might try to run off, and he was right. He also told me . . ." She broke off suddenly and looked embarrassed.

The Blairs' parents looked meaningfully at each other. Then their father faced Elenore Stewart squarely. "I'll thank you to tell me what you were going to say just now. What did Sir Guy also tell you? About me, was it?"

She laughed briefly. "What he said *was* that the shepherd at Mowdy Mains had a reputation for dispatching strange dogs and kicking the bottoms of strange folk off the hill in lambing time and that he was, for all that, a dashed fine shepherd. Only he didn't say 'bottoms' and he didn't say 'dashed', if you see what I mean. He also said he was afraid he might lose you, or have to lose you, by which I gather you might be planning to leave him."

Betsy held her breath to see what their parents would say to this open disclosure of what they had meant to keep to themselves.

"No me," said their father, looking away. "*I'm* no planning any such thing, and you can tell him that. If it's plans that are in the air, they're no mine. He'll have to look somewhere else for *plans*! Gardner? We've work to do."

With a nod to Elenore Stewart, he set off with Gardner at last. Meanwhile, Rannie, Jocky and Wee Nan had drifted over to the twins and were embarking on a few sillinesses that were their ritual in making friends. From her place by the gate, Betsy could hear a few comments about South America where the plums came from and was it true that the most famous mountain there was called Plum Duff? Rannie shoved Jocky and told him not to be daft and use his *sugar loaf*. The twins began to respond with a giggle and a duck of the head. But they didn't speak until Wee Nan, having studied them long and hard without getting anywhere, finally had to give in and ask, "Are you boys or girls?"

The twins looked at each other and pointed to each other, speaking at the same time.

"He's a boy."

"She's a girl."

Their accents were funny, anyway, but this perfect synchronisation of their answer made for as much confusion as before. Elenore Stewart came over and, stepping between them, put a hand on each. Looking at her right hand, she said, "This is Lucas. And this –" to her left hand "– is Philippa. In other words, Luke and Lippi. Now, you two, put Janey on her leash and off you go on home. Run! Double quick — your Uncle Guy will be worrying. I've got a stone in my shoe — I'll be right behind you!"

The twins trotted off along the road with their dog safely leashed.

Elenore Stewart leaned on the fence and lifted a foot to loosen the lace of her shoe. She talked as she went through the motions of ridding herself of some obstacle inside, though Betsy didn't hear anything drop when the shoe was shaken.

"Mrs Blair," the young woman was saying, "you have a cheery-looking family about you. D'you think those two young charges of mine might come and play sometimes? They need other children."

The Blairs, gathered round their mother now,

were listening closely. Their mother looked at them consideringly and gave Elenore Stewart her answer. "Oh aye. No bother at all. This lot'll soon make them feel at home. Eh? Will you no?" she said, consulting "this lot". They nodded willingly.

Elenore Stewart sighed, re-doing her lace. "You see, they've had to leave their home across the ocean, and they're quite homesick. It'll take time for them to adjust."

"I see. Poor wee souls! Well, send them up any time — maybe not with the dog, though, if you don't mind. My husband is very wrought up about today."

"Yes, of course. Actually, they get about on horseback most of the time. It'll be a nice ride up here for them. Thanks. I'm grateful to you."

"Eh — do they not have parents or something, I wonder?"

"No. No parents now, but something — in me. I'm a kind of cousin, trying to mother them. Gave up a tidy job in Rio, with a diplomat, to take them on. I sometimes think I've made a wretched mistake — not for myself but for *them*. I'd got used to a tidy life. Anyway, I mustn't keep you. I wonder . . . d'you think . . . may *I* come too sometimes . . . with Luke and Lippi?"

"That you may, and welcome."

Elenore Stewart smiled, hesitated a moment as though to ask yet another question that she was having trouble phrasing, and then, relaxing her brow, set off along the road with a wave. Betsy noticed that she still seemed to have a stone in her shoe but when she paid closer attention to the young woman's walk she realised that one leg looked less shapely than the other.

"Mum?" she asked as they turned indoors. "Is that woman sort of lame?"

"Aye. I thought she hirpled that wee bit. What bonnie bairns, too! Missing their home, she said." Betsy looked quickly at their mother, noting a woebegone drop in her voice at these last words. Their mother returned her look for a moment with an expression in her eyes that might have been pity — for the exiled twin children or for her own, Betsy couldn't tell. However, the subject of *their* uprooting was not mentioned further, their mother turning her attention to the immediate issue of the killer dog.

"I wonder how your father is getting on over there. Folk can be terrible close-mouthed in that village."

Betsy had a thought. "We could ask Mr Ross to ask the classes at school if they have any information. He did that about old Mrs Lauder's lost cat and it worked."

"Aye. The bairns'll talk whiles when their folk keep mum, right enough. Well, I better feed that lamb again. Listen, get Rannie and Jocky to make a pen with bales in the hayshed for it, and then you gather the eggs and feed the hens."

As she went about the allotted chores, Wee Nan

helping her, Betsy thought about the children from the Castle. Would they be joining the village school? Perhaps they would have a governess, the way old Sir Guy's family had when they were young, by all accounts. Or maybe they'd go to some boarding-school, though that seemed a cruel-like thing to do to them and them just trying to get used to a new home. They'd certainly not have their beloved Janey with them at a boarding-school. Not only that, they'd likely have to be *separated* from each other, since such schools took just boys or just girls. "It wouldn't do at all," she said out loud, placing warm eggs in the basket lined with straw.

"What won't, Betsy? What won't do?" asked Wee Nan at her side.

"Oh — I was just thinking about those twins."

"You mean Look Slippy?"

"What? Oh . . ." She laughed at Nan's pronounciation of the twins' names. "Yes. I was wondering what school they'd go to and how it wouldn't do to move them about any more."

"What's wrong with moving about?"

"Well . . . well, you know how we don't want to move from here, from Mowdy Mains?"

"Yes. Because Rannie says there's places and things still to explore?"

"Well, yes. Anyway, *I* think children should have a say about moving from places they like. *Jack* knows all about that. *Jack* could tell that woman!"

Betsy realised that Wee Nan, who'd known no

other place to live than Mowdy Mains, having been a toddler when the Blairs had first come there, was looking perplexed. Not wanting to worry her unduly with her own consternations, Betsy turned to the chore of feeding corn to the hens in the stackyard, Nan's special task.

It was a gladdening activity. All feeding of animals was, Betsy reflected. So was seeing them grow every day, like the lambs, and following their progress out to the Big Hill in time. And it was good to see the Big Hill itself change with the seasons and note the Hawthorn hedge by the dipper turn white another May. Friends, she thought, didn't have to be people. Some other kinds of friends were more reliable. *Rooted in one dear perpetual place* was a good way to put it. She couldn't remember who'd put it exactly, but Ireland vaguely seemed connected. Mr Ross lent her a lot of poetry books, some of them too hard for her, but lines often lingered like that one. Then she thought of the blown-down beech trees on the hill and she shivered.

3
Signs of an Unknown Enemy

The next Monday morning while walking over the hill to school with Jack Tattersall, who always joined them at the end of an old track called the Pony Road, the Blairs talked about Gardner's investigative round of the village with their father in an attempt to find the owner of the killer dog. There had been plenty of dogs, all right, but none had been out of their gardens that day. Bob Innis, the policeman, who knew every family, including cats, dogs, pet rabbits and budgies, declared it must have been some stranger's dog. He himself was as concerned about the attack on the sheep as Ewan Blair, for he did not care for such criminal mysteries in *his* territory. He felt it an attack on his guardianship of the village and, he said firmly, he'd make it his business to find out what he could.

"I wonder," Betsy said, stopping to let Nan catch up at the top of the hill, "if he's said anything to Mr Ross about making an announcement in Assembly."

"Aye," said Rannie, leaping over the fence, ignoring the stile. "The Heidie will soon find out who's behind it. He found out who was pinching everybody's dinner money, mind."

"No *everybody's*! Two laddies pinching each other's, you fool," Jocky corrected his brother, laughing.

Gardner was thoughtful. "It's not a bad idea to speak to Mr Ross. I'll do that."

Betsy turned to Jack. "Is Flo Jinty better?"

Flo Jinty was Jack's "adopted" grandmother. Until the Blairs made friends with her the previous summer, she had been an old, unknown recluse with the reputation of being a witch. Jack, a runaway from several so-called "homes" where he'd been put "into care", had managed not to be caught up with so far. The last welfare officer to find him had mysteriously vanished from the district, destroying Jack's file as well. Flo Jinty had given Jack refuge in her cottage last winter. They understood one another. When he wanted to spend time away, going to his tree-house in a clump of pines down Ballin Burn, she would wave him off with a bag of scones and bid him return soon. She had been ill with a chest cold recently and the Blairs' mother had sent a large bowl of soup home with Jack every day of the last week as he passed on his way from school. He'd carried it tied in a cloth slung on a stick over his shoulder — like people in fairy tales going off to seek their fortunes.

"She's up out of bed. She talks about wanting to come and see who it is that makes *sich fery good soop*," he said, imitating Flo Jinty's way of speaking. "I'll have to find a way of fetching her across that hill before . . ." He stopped.

Betsy knew what he was going to say. "Don't bother. Our mother can go to her, you know, now that she knows Flo Jinty would welcome folk."

"All the same, I'd still like to get her out of that little glen of hers sometimes. I was wondering about the Pony Road. Why's it called that?"

Gardner answered. "We drive the sheep along it to take them out to the Big Hill. It's aye been called the Pony Road because years ago, it seems, the shepherd at Mowdy Mains used to take feeding out to the sheep with a wee pony and cart. And I think they used to fetch peats in from the hill as well, once. Pity we don't have a pony and cart, eh?"

Jack nodded and, as they passed through the school gates with gathering numbers of village children, Betsy observed him looking at the tree-house that Mr Ross had had built, using Jack's personal model, in the big beech tree in the corner of the school playground.

That day there was hardly any need for Mr Ross's appeal in Assembly for any clues about the killer dog. Everybody already knew about the incident by the Blaeberry Burn and there were plenty of eager volunteers of information, not to Mr Ross but to the several members of the Blair family, at play-time, dinner-time, and home-time, not to mention whispered gems across the desks during class-time. It went on all week, the result being a totally useless, sometimes ridiculous collection of garbled "clues" that depressed the Blairs so much they didn't even bother to report any of it to their father.

They did, however, talk among themselves as they made their way home to Mowdy Mains at the end of the day.

"You might know Dannie Turner would have something to say!" scoffed Rannie, Dannie Turner being the greatest nuisance in his life. "D'you know what he said? He said *he* saw *six* killer dogs streaking up on to our hill last Sunday, *and* he saw them all coming back down, slavering and covered with blood. Brainless idiot!"

"Lena Drummond came and told *me* a kind of queer tale," Gardner said.

"What queer tale?" they all wanted to know.

"She said Dick Baxter skinned his knuckles on some rope at the train station doing a scout's knot one night and some dog smelled the blood and bit off one of his fingers."

"Listen," declared Rannie, "Dick canny even tie his *shoelaces* right, never mind scouts' knots. The only thing tied about *him* is his tongue, for he hardly speaks to anybody – just walks about with his hands in his pockets and his head in the clouds, shoelaces whipping about his ankles. Mind, he's awful good at long sums in his head. Anyway, what dog?"

"I told you it was a queer tale," Gardner went on. "She said she got it from Robbie Stark, who had it from Big Malcolm Bailey, who got it from some other body. So I just went and asked Dick himself. And what *he* said was far different."

They waited.

Gardner picked his way across the Swanshie Bit (a permanent patch of bog across the path) before stopping to tell them. "What he *actually* said was that his uncle's rope factory has two trained Alsatian dogs on patrol all night, and one's gone missing! Case of Chinese whispers, see?"

They were at first so amused by the hilarious transformation in Dick Baxter's whispered comment in class that they hardly paid attention to the meaning of it. Jack soon reminded them.

"Well, maybe if they could find that missing dog they'll have found the killer," he suggested.

"Aye," agreed Gardner, "I thought of that. But that rope factory is five miles up the coast. If the beast ran away, say, there are fields and flocks far nearer than this for it to make for. Why *our* land and *our* sheep?"

It was a disturbing thought. They walked on in silence, eager to be home, hungry for the bowls of soup and bread waiting at the end of the school day. As they approached, their mother emerged from the house to bring Jack his bowl. Thanking her again, he set off along the Pony Road which he'd follow for some way before heading off to Ballin Brae and Flo Jinty's place.

Whether or not Gardner, Rannie and Jocky had the same worried thoughts as her, Betsy noted that, like herself, nobody seemed to want to talk about them and certainly not to ask their parents what *they* thought. Tea-time was a rather quiet meal. Normally, their mother would have noticed their unaccustomed quietness and teased out the matter. But she was, herself, preoccupied — or perhaps she knew the matter had to do with her own trouble at the moment and had no heart for telling over painful mysteries without solutions.

However, Betsy told them over in her own mind as she lay in bed that night beside Wee Nan who was already asleep. If, as their father had hinted to that Elenore Stewart, there were "plans" in the air regarding their moving out of Mowdy Mains, plans that weren't *his*, whose plans were they? And why? What if the missing patrol dog from Dick Baxter's uncle's rope factory *was* the sheep killer? As Gardner had pointed out, why had it run across five miles of sheep country before starting its worrying? She wondered if the sheep-killing and those "plans" their father had spoken about were connected in some way. If they were, it all pointed to something more than mere plans, something more in the nature of hostile conspiracy by persons unknown. If these "persons unknown" existed, who could they be? Why were they hostile? And – Betsy's mind jolted awake from its drowsy wonderings, as the question struck her – *what would they do next?*

She felt afraid and wished she could go to their parents with her fear. But she had the feeling that they were as perplexed and even as afraid as she was. She almost longed for one of their plain, straightforward "crabbit days" filled with minor crises easily solved, instead of this sense of doom building up to goodness knows what. Wearied, she fell asleep, half aware of their own dog, Young Laird, giving a growl before quiet descended on Mowdy Mains.

4
Sheep's Clothing

Betsy woke up to the sound of repeated bleating beneath her window. Nan was up, looking out.

"Daddie's skinning a lamb," she reported.

They watched together the operation taking place outside in the stackyard. Called "setting on", it was something they were used to seeing quite often in lambing time, but even so the end result had a certain *un*certainty about it that made for close watching.

In the Wee Field beyond the stackyard and right by the fence of it paced a ewe, back and forth, back and forth, bleating for the dead lamb that Ewan Blair was handling, screened from her by his body. In a few minutes, with some deft movements of his horn-handled lambing-knife, he had removed the dead lamb's skin just as it was, slimy and wet from its fatal birth. Now he laid the little coat in a pile on the grass, covering the red-raw remains of the lamb with his canvas lambing-bag until it could be buried.

He disappeared into one of the steading sheds and reappeared carrying a live lamb in his arms, one of a pair of healthy two-day-old twins. Next he took the dead lambskin and, cutting holes in the appropriate places, he draped it over the live lamb, putting its legs through the holes so that it wore the coat securely. All the while, the mother sheep continued to bleat. Betsy and Nan stood at the window, eager to see the outcome, to see if the deception would work yet another time.

Their father carried the disguised lamb over to the bereaved mother. She ran away at his approach, but only so far, and then she turned and stamped her foot, angry at having to run away from what she was instinctively and powerfully drawn to. The lamb, now over the fence and in the field with her, tottered towards her bleating, emitting its own little quaver of a bleat in response. Ewe and lamb came together. She sniffed round and round it, pushing with her muzzle. Something wasn't right, and yet . . . Her own smell was on the lamb, strong and definite, and yet . . . Her head went up. She sniffed the air, then the lamb again. It tried to nuzzle under fleece, seeking to suck. But she wasn't satisfied. At their window, Betsy and Nan kept watch, doubtful now. Their father, too, leaning on the gate, watched quietly at a safe distance from the mother and the lamb.

Finally, as nearly always happened, instinctual needs overcame subtle reservations. The lamb's need to suckle and the ewe's need to mother came together. In a day or two, when the original smell and the new had blurred into each other, it would be all right to remove the dried lambskin and the "trick" of "setting on" would be complete. Meanwhile, the mother of the twins, ill-supplied with milk for *two* offspring, would now be able to provide very well for her remaining one.

"There. She's taken it," murmured Wee Nan. "I thought for a minute she wasn't going to. I'm glad now."

Betsy agreed. "Sometimes, when they don't, Dad has to take the skin off again and pour cold tea all over the lamb and make the ewe drink some."

"Why?"

"To make *her* smell match the smell of the lamb. That usually works. Come on! Time we fed the hens."

Downstairs, they found their mother just in from milking the cows. She was busy sieving the milk through a muslin cloth into a large milk basin. As she carried it full through to the milkhouse, a cool, narrow room with its net-screened window open to the air and long table against one wall, she said over her shoulder, "Scones in the oven, Betsy. Tea's made."

Betsy fetched the scones to the kitchen table already set with butter, jam, and slices of yellow cheese. "Where're the boys?"

Their mother came back to the sink and began to wash and sterilize the milking utensils with boiling water. "Oh, they've been sent out to the hill."

"What for?"

"Young Laird. He's run away again. Your father's no very pleased. He thought he had him trained not to do that any more. Anyway, the boys're away to see if they can find him. I just hope they do, for it'll be a hopeless task trying to run this place with just the one dog. What your father'll be like attempting it doesn't bear thinking about!"

Betsy looked anxiously at their mother's back where she bent over the sink, steam from the kettle rising round her elbows. She did wish a little that their mother wouldn't always be so prepared ahead of time to have to face their father's ill-humour when things went wrong. Sometimes, there was no need for worry. Betsy wondered if their mother did this kind of thing *in order to* ward off bad luck. While she was thinking about the problem, their father came in asking for some dry stockings.

He sat down by the stove to loosen the laces of his boots. He was clearly deep in thought, for he kept losing his place in the loosening process and even began to tighten them again when he'd got half-way down the series of criss-crosses. Nobody said anything. Suddenly, he looked at Wee Nan wonderingly. She went on eating her scone quietly, returning his look with a little expectant smile.

"Did you," he said finally, not frowning or anything but sounding stern, "by any chance open Young Laird's kennel door and not shut it again?"

"When?" Wee Nan asked.

"What d'you mean *when*? *Any* time. This morning. Last night. Did you?"

Betsy saw that her sister was going blank, the way she remembered doing herself on those occasions when their father fired a series of stern questions at her. "She never went near his kennel last night, Dad. And she's just newly up. Why?"

"What about you? Did you see the door no snecked?"

"*No!* Why?"

"Well, he was out when I went to get him early this morning. I'll tell you this much, he never let himself out! That door wasn't shut right. Gardner swears *he* shut it after he fed the dogs last thing at night. Rannie and Jocky both say *they* never touched it." He looked at their mother and shrugged.

"Well," she said quietly, handing him a dry pair of knitted stockings, "*I'm* certainly in the clear, for I've no call to go near the kennels, with Gardner in total charge."

"Aye," he answered, "there's a fishy smell about it."

Betsy and Nan followed him out to have a look at the empty kennel. He opened the other one, calling Trim out to him. She was an older dog, not as quick as Young Laird, but steady and competent.

Wee Nan stood by the empty kennel. "Is that the fishy smell you mean, Daddie?" she asked.

About to depart with Trim to look his sheep, he hesitated at her question. Like all of them in the family, when Nan said something that wasn't immediately understood, he knew to pay closer attention. She often noticed things that passed by the others.

"What smell?"

Nan stuck her head right inside Young Laird's kennel and sniffed. "*That* smell. It's not nice. I've never smelt it before. Have you, Betsy?"

Betsy had a sniff. "Hm. Moth balls?"

There father came over. He bent down and put his head inside the little shed. Betsy watched his face turning from a curious frown to grim recognition. He felt about in the bedding straw, lifting his hand to smell several times. Then he found what he sought — a small, crushed piece of cotton wool. He smelled it and turned his head away with closed eyes. "Aye," he said. "Ether. Plain as daylight."

He stepped away, putting his find in his jacket pocket, and stood looking away from Mowdy Mains' high place across the fields and woods stretching down to where they met the waters of the Firth. He looked beyond all that to the far green islands lying on the horizon with their peaked mountains very clear that day.

"What is it, Dad?" Betsy asked. She knew what ether was but she wanted to know what he was making of this "fishiness". But all he said, before moving off to his work with a weary swing of his arm, was again, "As daylight."

Betsy was left with her own dread thoughts and the conviction that she should probably try to divert Wee Nan from the incident for the moment.

"Those hens," she said, "will go on egg-strike if we don't look slippy."

Nan laughed and skipped to grasp Betsy's hand. "D'you think they'll come and play today?"

"Who?"

"*Them*. Look Slippy."

"Oh, the twins! Would you like that, then?"

"Yes. I'd like to show them our *Bonnie Beech Bark*."

Betsy noted the name. So that's what it was to be, then. They proceeded to the grain shed to fetch feeding for the hens already gathered in a flock by the accustomed door from which their food was thrown to them twice a day. They were making melancholy, questioning caws as they paced slowly about the yard, waiting. The morning feed was just corn. In the evening they had a mash made from cooked potato peelings, oatmeal and water, mixed with suitable scraps gathered from the day's cooking.

Betsy opened the corn sack. "We're nearly at the bottom of this. I don't see a new bag, either."

She reported this to their mother after they'd seen to the hens and was surprised to learn that they might have to get rid of some hens, as that was the last of the corn now.

"Can we not get some more from Weaver the Grieve? I'll go down with Nan and get some. Just a wee bag to be going on with, like? Eh? In Nan's old pushchair?"

Their mother lifted the pie she'd been crimping

and put it into the oven. She straightened up, wiping her floury hands on her apron. "Well, he told your father there was no more corn for us. And it's too dear to buy."

"Oh. Did you not *buy* it from him, then?"

"No. Your father and him had an arrangement, but don't ask me about it now. All I know is, something's gone wrong with it, and there's no more corn forthcoming for the hens or feeding for the cows either. I wish we'd never got to depend on that Ty Weaver." She sat down at the kitchen table with a sigh. "He was such a help, too, when he first came here. We were just finding our feet ourselves. Oh, well, maybe it's not his fault at that. All the same . . ." She was half talking to herself. None of it made any sense to Betsy.

Suddenly, their mother became brisk, taking hold of herself. "Listen! I need some things from the village. If the two of you go now you'll be back in time for dinner. Away you go, now. Here's the money. Here's the wee list. Don't forget the clothes pins! That last gale broke half of what I had."

Glad to be of practical use, with a clear task, instead of being troubled by unclear problems, Betsy got their mother's large burlap shopping bag from its peg behind the scullery door. Nan carried her own miniature version and together they set off. With Nan in tow, it would be a walk full of little rests, but it didn't matter, Betsy thought. It was a clear, sunny day. The air above was "larky", the way she loved it, enough to lift the spirits considerably.

They reached the top of the hill where the view was so splendid. Before them, the Firth's broad blue expanse sparkled. Behind lay the moor and the fields of Mowdy Mains dotted with sheep. Betsy turned to look back and noticed the group of three figures returning home. Gardner, Rannie and Jocky were coming back from their hunt for Young Laird and were, as far as she could make out, dogless.

"Can I sit on the Sea Serpent for a while?" asked Nan, running to the dry-stone dyke that marked the border between Mowdy Mains land here and the fields of the neighbouring farm that was called The Howe where Ty Weaver and his wife had their living. This was the chief farm of the Kilsmore estate now, not so much because it had more land than Mowdy Mains or Black Hill or Ballin Farm (which were mainly sheep farms) but because it was dairy and arable and brought in a richer income. It employed four dairymen, two ploughmen, and sundry other farm workers who lived in cottages set round a small cobbled square attached to the steading. Ty Weaver acted as overall manager or "grieve" for The Howe and its people. Betsy, who knew several of the children from the Square, had heard them say, quoting their parents, that Ty Weaver didn't know the first thing about farming and God knew how he'd got the job of grieve but they were stuck with him.

She followed Nan over to the Sea Serpent, so called because the neat, regularly spaced top stones reminded her sister of the neck scales of a sea serpent in her *Rupert* annual. She was wondering what sort of "arrangement" their father had had with Weaver the Grieve. She'd realised soon after they'd moved to Mowdy Mains that their father's attitude towards The Howe was somewhat different from the way he thought of the other farms on the estate. With Matt Fleming from Black Hill and with Geordie Rutherford from Ballin Farm he seemed comfortable. But any mention of Weaver the Grieve seemed, now she came to think on it more deeply, tinged with unease perhaps? Certainly, there was a difference. Was it that Ty Weaver was in a position of some authority over the three shepherds? Perhaps he wasn't really, but had tried to be? That wouldn't sit well with the shepherd at Mowdy Mains, Betsy knew. Their father detested anyone "coming it" with him, as he called it, especially if, as might be the case with Ty Weaver, they didn't know the first thing about the matter in hand.

"Come on, Nan. Down you get."

She was helping Nan off the back of the Sea Serpent, still thinking about Weaver the Grieve, when she saw the man himself walking along the side of the field to their left, coming towards them. For a moment, she worried he might be about to give them a row for climbing on his dyke like that, but he nodded affably enough as he drew near.

"Aye." He gave the customary greeting in these parts. "That you going messages for your mother, eh?"

He was a tall, rangy man and he wore blue overalls tucked into a pair of rubber boots. He didn't walk with a stick like the shepherds, a mark of their calling, and perhaps that was why Betsy always got the impression that he was somehow aimless, unpurposeful, idle. What he did have, slung on his shoulder, was a pair of fieldglasses. Also, Betsy noted, he had on a short, sleeveless sheepskin jacket over his jumper, the fleece-side out. For a daft moment it put her in mind of the lambskin coat their father had fashioned earlier that day for the "setting on". The thought coloured her response to his question about their errand.

"Yes," she said, moving away with Wee Nan by the hand, "and we better hurry up."

He watched them, benevolently smiling. "How're the hens doing? Laying all right, eh?"

Betsy gave an automatic answer in her wish to get going. "Yes, thanks."

"Tell your mother I asked, mind."

"I'll tell her. Come on, Nan. Cheerio, Mr Weaver."

"Aye."

As they hurried down the path on the other side of the hill, through ferns and heather and round by the reservoir that was the village water supply, Betsy only now remembered something else she'd heard said about Ty Weaver, by Lena Drummond, in fact, who lived at the Square. Lena had said her mother thought he'd been "a bit of a wolf in his young days" before he came to The Howe.

Betsy considered that phrase, "a bit of a wolf", and her mind, prompted by his appearance, supplied the natural follow-on "in sheep's clothing". Such people, she knew, weren't to be trusted.

5

Stravaiging Away from Troubles

On their return to Mowdy Mains at mid-day, Betsy found that, as she'd expected, the boys had had no luck in their search on the hill for Young Laird. Also, when their father got in from his round of the place, he too had seen no trace of the runaway.

"We're no meant to find him that easy, if at all," they heard him murmur to their mother as she bent over his shoulder placing a dish of potatoes on the table. "But I'm blowed if I'll give up, even if they're out to get me one way or another."

"Who, Dad?" Rannie asked loudly. "Who's out to get you?"

Their father frowned at him. "Never you mind. Get on wi' your soup, the lot of you."

Betsy sighed to herself. She knew at times like this that children were meant to be deaf, dumb and totally incurious, and yet it seemed to her to be asking a lot of them when their parents engaged in such anxiety-loaded conversations. The only thing to do was listen all the harder for clues. It was certainly the kind of situation where you had to be very careful and not pry so much that the adults would clam up completely and talk only when thoroughly alone. The trouble was that if what you overheard didn't make sense, it was tempting to fill in and invent so that it *did*. There was always the chance that you'd make a total hash of the truth — like the story of Dick Baxter's skinned knuckles that weren't! Betsy wished her parents would speak plain to their children, but no. Here they were now, being told yet again never to mind. All at once, it made her angry.

"Well, *why*," she asked, spearing a potato from the dish and adding it to her soup, "why do we have to move from Mowdy Mains? *We* don't want to go. What's the reason for *that*? Don't tell us never to mind about *that*!"

Everybody looked at her first and then quickly at their father.

"Oh?" he said, surveying their faces, in a tone that suggested he'd just learned something remarkable about them in that moment, something that amused rather than angered him. "O-oh? So you want to know that, eh? Well, so you will. I'll give it to you in one word. Money. Money's the reason. There y'are!"

It was a reason that required no further questioning. They all knew that "money", given as a reason, meant "*not enough* money". Betsy recalled their mother's comment earlier in the day about feeding for the hens and cows being "too dear". If they didn't manage to find Young Laird, their father would be obliged to purchase a new sheepdog, and they cost a lot of money. Clearly, whoever had removed him from his kennel with the aid of that ether pad must have known this. Perhaps they'd stolen him in order to sell him for a good price somewhere far from the district. Betsy had heard of such sheepdog-stealing happening in England. Maybe there was a gang operating up and down the country. In any case, it all went back to money, all right, and the need or greed for it.

"Mummy?" Nan's voice broke in. "Yon Mr Weaver was asking how the hens were today. He said to tell you he was asking, so I am."

Their mother, on her feet about to clear away empty plates, suddenly sat down again. Their father pushed back his chair, holding the edge of the table at arm's length, and looked at their mother searchingly. Neither spoke a word, but to Betsy they were the very picture of consternation and unquiet, as though this kindly enquiry from the grieve were, on the contrary, full of menace!

The strain of not knowing what was going on in the adult world was too much for Rannie. He grabbed a last potato from the dish with his fingers and said loudly,

"Come a riddle, come a riddle, come a rot, tot, tot
A wee wee man in a red red coat
A stick in his hand an' a stane in his throat
Come a riddle, come a riddle, come a rot, tot, tot.
What is it? *A CHERRY!*"

He answered himself with exaggerated triumph and sped away from the table, through the scullery, and out into the stackyard. His performance startled the others out of their stoney puzzlement and seemed to bring their parents, too, as it were, to their senses.

Their father laughed openly, though briefly. "That's telling *us* off, eh?" he said to their mother who bit her lip, half smiling. He turned to his other children and, with a nod towards the window and the road leading away from the farm, he said, "Away and play. Me and your mother, have we no aye taken care of you? And so we will still. Away and play. Look! Yonder's the bairns from the Castle coming along the road. There's Rannie running to meet them. Galloping, more like."

At the window to look, Jocky remarked, "They're on their ponies. And Rannie's on his! Look at him belting away at his hip! I'm away out."

By the time Gardner, Betsy and Nan had got to the visitors beyond the farm gate, Rannie and Jocky had somehow managed to replace the twins in the saddles and, in a matter of seconds from gaining this position, Rannie had managed to get himself tossed smartly into a clump of rushes by the roadside. Betsy ran to him in alarm but he was up and ready to have another go.

"Wait!" she cried. "*Wait*, you daft thing! That horse doesn't know you yet. Give it time. You don't just hop on and away you go, you know. Look, Jocky's stuck as well. Ponies are choosy."

Jocky's mount simply refused to move and was clearly set on cropping the grass for the rest of the day. The twins watched with identical, knowing smiles. Betsy realised that her cautions to Rannie had really been her way of telling the twins that she recognised that *they* were the real, true masters and that such loyalty from the ponies (namely, throwing Rannie and ignoring Jocky) was a fine thing. She wasn't sure why she wanted the twins to get this message — unless it was something to do with belonging, something she sensed would be a help to two youngsters far from home.

"Look Slippy," Wee Nan's voice came from behind them. Both twins looked round at the name, then at each other and laughed. Nan went shy for a moment, then remembered what she wanted to ask them. "Where's Janey?"

It was, Betsy reflected, quite remarkable, the way those two looked alike and *moved* alike. They each, at the same moment, took Nan by the hand, sharing their answer.

"She's at home today —"
"— with Elenore —"
"— and Uncle Guy —"
"— getting used to —"
"— her new kennel."

Nan looked from one to the other, delighted with the phenomenon they made. In their turn, they seemed very taken with the smallest Blair and with the inspired name she'd called them.

"Hey!" Rannie was feeding one of the horses with a handful of long, sweet grass. "Look at this. She's eating from my hand. She's getting to know me."

Look Slippy looked. "It's not a her —"

"— it's a him."

Rannie took a quick look underneath. "Oh aye, so it is. What's his name, then?"

"Carlos, and —"

"— the other one's Carmen."

Gardner was stroking Carmen's white blaze. "South American?"

"Yes, they're called —"

"— after people we liked there."

Look Slippy looked sadly at the ground. However, they weren't allowed to do it for long. "Come on!" Rannie said. "Come on, we'll go over to Ballin Brae and see Jack."

Look Slippy seemed hesitant. "Who's that? Is it —"

"— far to go?"

Jocky began, "Jack's a great boy and —"

"— no, it's no *that* far," finished Rannie. Then *he* began, as he leapt over the ditch, leading the way hillwards, "Over the hills and a great way off —"

"— Get on your pony and dinny fall off!" finished Jocky, speeding after his brother.

Look Slippy's faces brightened at their manner being copied with such obvious liking. In a moment, with identical mounting movements, they were into their saddles and were picking their way across the hill, making for the Pony Road after Rannie and Jocky. Then, again with one accord, twin faces turned round to the less boisterous Blairs and twin voices said, "Coming?"

The gesture pleased Betsy enormously, for although it was clear that Look Slippy had been instantly drawn to Rannie and Jocky, they showed they were also aware of the quieter qualities of the others and of the regard which Wee Nan had shown for them. It would have been easy to go galloping off with the breeze after the boys, but they didn't. Betsy had sometimes wondered what made some children show instant feeling for others and some children very little. It perhaps had something to do with intelligence. But it wasn't *clever* intelligence, like being a star at arithmetic. She felt sure it was connected with knowing about sadness, too.

The twins were racing their steeds along the old Pony Road past Rannie and Jocky, turning with a flourish to wait and then going on, and gradually slowing to a companionable amble, so that the boys could walk alongside and give the occasional pat.

"It's too bad," Gardner murmured, getting down on his hunkers for Nan to climb on his back for her customary piggy-back on the way to Ballin Brae, "that the twins will only have a few months of our rare company, eh?"

Betsy agreed. "Still, Jack'll be here. There's that."

They moved, wandering like a small flock across the hill, hair, loose jumpers, pony manes, and (in Rannie's case) elbow tatters blowing in the wind that always came off the farthest reaches of the moor.

At length, they reached the ridge above the little

glen where Flo Jinty's cottage stood with Ballin Brae at its back. Green ferns grew round the walls beside clumps of broom. In front, cropping the grass to a neat length that gave the place a tidy look, was Clover, the once-demented but now-contented cow that Flo Jinty had kept, courtesy of Matt Fleming of Black Hill who'd owned her for the little while of her madness. The burn's water was plentiful and the two ponies needed little urging down the slope after their trek through the heather. The sound of their splashing hooves and the hails of the children brought Flo Jinty to her door.

"Ach, 'tiss the lot of you!" she exclaimed in her soft accent. "You will be looking for your friend, I suppose. He went out an hour past and he wass hoping to see you, too. Haf you not seen sign of him? Well, now, you had better stay close till he comes back, for fear you miss each other again. Wait you there!"

She turned slowly in the doorway and went inside, returning in a few minutes with a small basket of buns which she held out to Betsy, waving it away from herself, as though taking it was doing her a great favour. "There now! There's two for each of you, with enough to give one to the little horses there."

It was her greeting to Look Slippy and they returned her welcome with a double "thank you". For the moment, it was enough.

Nan came and sat on the doorstep in the sunshine,

warm in the little glen, shielded from the wind. "Blaeberry buns are my best food," she said, giving Flo Jinty's leg a cuddle through its long skirt, "and you are the best bun-maker."

"Iss that so? And haf you eaten so many plaeperry puns in your life, maidie?"

"No. Just these —"

"Well!"

"— but it *feels* the way I said!"

"Oh, *feels*, does it, now?"

There was a little silence while everyone savoured the splendid buns. Then Look Slippy commented, from horseback.

"Actually, *we've* had blueberry muffins —"

"— many times, and —"

"— these here really are —"

"— the best, actually."

Flo Jinty put her hands to her cheeks, giving her head a little shake.

"Ach, now I believe it!" she laughed. The reception of Look Slippy into her particular fold of friendship was given a great boost. It was the pleasantest thing to see. It occurred to Betsy that in Flo Jinty too, as in Jack, the twins would have good companions to go to when the Blairs had to leave.

But where *was* Jack? Rannie had clambered to the top of a nearby birch whose slender branches scarcely held him, and now he called down, "There he's! Hey, Tattie Bogle!"

He began to wave wildly while retracing his

upward clamber, one stage of which meant swinging across a wide space between two spreading branches. He missed his footing, grabbed successfully the end of one of the branches and while everyone waited to hear the ominous crack and see him crash to the ground with at least one broken leg, the tree let its silver-barked arm bend in a merciful bow that lowered him gently to earth. Jocky cast one wondering glance at the birch as he followed his brother, while the others went on marvelling for some time at the timely flexibility of one of the most beautiful, though most frail-looking of trees thereabouts.

Betsy was thinking of a poem she'd come across in one of Mr Ross's books about a boy that swings on birches. One line said, "One could do worse than be a swinger of birches." At the time she'd read it she'd been put in mind of Rannie, all right, and here he'd actually done the thing, although not on purpose.

She turned to find Jack, flanked by Rannie and Jocky, labouring up the burnside with a bundle of wooden planks on his shoulder. "What's he going to do with that lot, I wonder?" she murmured to Gardner who was training his old fieldglasses on some spot beyond the far bank. Wee Nan had gone indoors with Flo Jinty for a drink of milk. Look Slippy, still mounted, were watching the approaching trio with interest.

"Heron," murmured Gardner.

"Let's see," she said.

He lowered the glasses. "There he goes."

The big grey bird, its neck tucked in and long legs trailing, flapped slowly downstream. Jack came up to the cottage wall and dumped his bundle.

"Did you see the heron? He fishes up this way every day, but I've seen his nest further down, past the *Bonnie Beech Bark*, it is. Did you see him? He's a beauty!"

He rubbed his unloaded shoulder and directed his question at Look Slippy who were staring at him rather lengthily. "Did *you* see the heron?"

They nodded, continuing to stare, craning their necks round when Carlos and Carmen tried to face them in another direction in pursuit of new grass by the burn. Jack, in his turn, was staring at the ponies with something like longing. Or was it calculation? He looked over at the twins, saying in a low voice to Betsy, "Are they the Castle kids? How'd you tell them apart?"

"You don't. One's Lucas, one's Lippi. Nan's christened them together as Look Slippy and they don't seem to mind. Why're they staring at *you* so much?" she said, equally low.

"Never seen anything like *me* before, probably," he joked.

"No. It's as if they *had*. Might as well ask. Come on. Come and meet them properly."

Look Slippy chose this moment to dismount at last, winding reins round a clump of broom. They strode straight to Jack, examining him with their blue eyes travelling from his hair to his chin.

"You look like —"

"— someone we used to play with."

"Oh? Where was that, then?" he asked.

"In our other home —"

"— in South America. D'you have —"

"— relatives or something there?"

Jack shook his head, laughing at their turnabout way of speaking. "I don't have relatives or anything *anywhere*," he said. "I have to adopt them — like this flock here, and Flo Jinty in the cottage there. Listen!" He turned to Gardner and the others leaning on the cottage wall, listening indeed. "Are they not the lucky ones, having horses, eh? Are they going to our school, by the way? Are you going to the village school?" he asked the twins.

They nodded, then added, "D'you wish you —"

"— had a horse?"

"Do I just!"

Look Slippy looked at each other, then slowly back at Jack, but said nothing further.

It was getting late. There was still a lot to show to their new friends, like the *Bonnie Beech Bark* riding at permanent anchor lower down the burn, the fallen row of beeches on the hill behind Mowdy Mains, Jack's wonderful tree-house, not to mention other parts of the moor they themselves had not yet explored, like the Mallard Loch they'd heard about somewhere. It was said to be in the middle of the moor past the treacherous haggs, those black bogs that even the sheep steered clear of. There was also a stand of pines that could be seen at the very top of Ballin Brae behind Flo Jinty's cottage that only Jack had been to so far. He'd not said much about it and the Blairs had got the idea that this was a place he wanted to keep private perhaps, but someday — someday before they left the district — surely they'd be granted a look at it.

Flo Jinty's small figure appeared at the door once more.

"Jack. It's time you were hungry, iss it not? Betsy, your mother will be out calling for you all, I doubt. Off home with you, now! Give your mother my kind regards."

They set off for Mowdy Mains. Rannie achieved his wish to ride Carlos without mishap, taking turns with Jocky, while Gardner, invited to try Carmen, surprised them all with his easy management of the horse, but then Gardner's gentle nature always won animals to him. Look Slippy seemed happy to share the task of carrying Nan when she flagged.

Betsy walked behind thoughtfully. She'd meant to ask Jack about those planks. He'd looked so purposeful, carrying them, and they were apparently the latest in a series of loads because she remembered that he'd thrown them down on top of a fair sized pile that was already there by the cottage wall. Jack, the architect of tree-houses, was up to something, for sure.

6

Night Boat to Morlie Bay

It was early in June when Mr Ross, who taught Betsy, Gardner and Jack, reminded the class of his intention to take some of them to visit the place where he had a boat moored in a sea-cave, a boat that he himself spent weekends in from time to time. He was one of those teachers who believe that the best kind of learning is from first-hand experience, preferably outside the classroom. To this end he had taken small groups of pupils to visit a working windmill, a travellers' encampment of hand-painted, horse-drawn caravans and tents, a castle with a moat and drawbridge, and now it was to be a lighthouse.

Each group would return and tell the rest of the class about their excursion, drawing pictures, writing commentaries and generally communicating their experience through all the skills they had — painting, writing, cartography, oral commentary, photography, and model-making. Mr Ross kept the excursions roughly within the boundaries of the local county, for he also believed that children who learn to know their own district well develop a desirable sense of place and of variety.

He was very keen on weather, too. That spring he'd taken down his months-old frieze that read

THE WORLD IS SO FULL OF A NUMBER OF THINGS and had replaced it with:

ALL SORTS OF THINGS AND WEATHER
MUST BE TAKEN IN TOGETHER
TO MAKE UP A YEAR.

Underneath, in tiny letters and bracketed, was the name *Emerson*, some poet from America. Reports from the excursions were expected to cover in detail aspects of the weather on that day. Mr Ross did not wait for ordinary fine days at all, the way most people do for outings, but seemed to welcome for the pupils the very experience of weather itself. As he was heard to say, you can exclude so much by too close planning and there was a valuable skill to be learned from managing matters as they came. Because of this attitude of his, which some folk called being "away for ile withoot a can", his excursions were often unpredictable. It was funny, really, because not being prepared in advance for something special, you were *actually* prepared for *anything*.

The group selected to visit Morlie Bay lighthouse, then, consisted of Betsy, Gardner, Jack, Lena Drummond, Dick Baxter, Robbie Stark and his sister Helen, and wee Andy Kyle, the postie's son. They'd been told to ask their parents for two lots of sandwiches each, with some apples and maybe some chocolate. They'd to dress however they liked, but anoraks were positively suggested, as were an extra pair of socks.

They were to leave, not bright and early that Saturday morning, but late in the day, after tea-time.

"I wish it was me that was going!" Rannie complained, watching Gardner packing his bag. Betsy started to say his turn would come, but then remembered that, as things stood, Rannie wouldn't have Mr Ross next year.

"Well, it's good you're no — in case the twins come up to play. They'll need you here," she consoled him.

Their father, who'd still not found any trace of Young Laird in the two weeks since he'd been gone, added, "Aye, and *I'll* need him to help *me* wi' the lambs I've to mark, seeing his brother's away gallivanting God knows where!"

Betsy glanced at Gardner who kept his eyes cast down at the task of packing his school-bag with the necessaries for their trip. "We'll be back tomorrow afternoon, Dad," she said. "It's not that long."

"Aye," their father went on, "I could do wi' starting the morn's morn, all the same, if the weather keeps up."

"If the weather keeps up," their mother said, listening to the damper being put on the lighthouse visit, "we'd *all* do ourselves a bit of good by going away for the day. That's what *I'm* thinking. Other folk do it, why no us?"

"Don't talk to *me* about other folk!" their father replied gruffly, his mind having been cleverly focussed on the real reason for his ill-humour. The fact was that another attack had been made on the sheep that very week, this time on the remotest part of the hill, called the Back of the World, where the boundary road with the next county ran.

There had been even fewer clues this time, for no one had seen or heard anything, and the gory evidence had been discovered at early light by a hill walker who'd strayed rather far from his path. He'd reported it to the nearest police station in Greenbeg, a town in the next county, but the constable who came to see Ewan Blair about the matter was able to give him little hope of finding the culprit, man or beast. From listening to odd snatches of talk between their parents, Betsy and Gardner had gathered that, having heard about the other incident of sheep-worrying and the loss of Young Laird, the Greenbeg constable had asked their parents if they had an enemy. Usually, when sheep were being worried in a district, it wasn't confined to any one stock like this. Even one rogue fox could cause havoc on several places at once. However, this wasn't the work of a fox, but of a large, powerful dog. It was a mystery what such an animal would be doing out at Back of the World where there was no village, no houses at all, and people rarely passed that way during the week.

After the constable's visit, Gardner and Betsy had noticed that their father had seemed increasingly on edge, while their mother looked at him in a funny sort of way, almost as though she felt to blame for their situation. Once, Betsy came upon them in the byre, their mother in tears against the flank of the cow she was milking, their father down on his hunkers telling her, "I know fine you'd nothing to do wi' it. We'll go. That's all."

Because there seemed to be some sort of strangeness between *them*, Betsy fled from knowing more. But the scene and the words had stamped themselves painfully in her mind.

The overnight excursion with Mr Ross came as a welcome relief from troubles, anyway. Betsy thought their father might actually be somewhat envious of the capacity his children had for shedding cares so easily when he couldn't. Perhaps that's what their mother saw in his sour comment to Gardner and that was why she was suggesting he take the day off, for fun.

"Anyway," she heard him saying, "where can we go? It costs money to go anywhere."

"No if we walk," their mother was replying. "The bairns know places."

Betsy and Gardner left the house at last to meet up with Jack as usual at the end of the Pony Road, leaving Rannie to sort out the best places to go on foot, if a day off was indeed in the air.

"Jack must be tired," said Betsy, watching their friend tramping to meet them at a slower pace than usual.

"No wonder. He walks twice as far as the rest of us any day."

However, at the sight of them and sharing their anticipation of the coming trip, Jack's face brightened with pleasure. He hailed them and broke into a trot, weariness dispelled. "Am I late?"

"On time."

Half an hour later they stood on the pier with their other classmates, waiting for Mr Ross to appear. Everyone was looking along the shore road to catch sight of him, but they suddenly heard his voice calling them from behind — from the water by the pier! And there, below them, was the man himself looking up at their astonished faces from the motor boat in which he was standing.

"Down you come, then! Careful on the steps, there. We don't want to start with a drookin', you know."

Wee Andy Kyle ran to be first down the flight of wet, slippery stone steps that had been built into the wall of the pier and he very nearly paid the penalty for his haste, landing on his bottom on the third step. He took the last steps with exceeding care, and Betsy remarked to herself that Andy Kyle looked to be made in the same mould as Rannie Blair and would probably need watching.

"Is this an oarie boat, sir?" asked Robbie Stark, who'd noticed the set of oars lying along one of the seats.

"Not while the motor works for us, but if we have any trouble with it, then yes, this'll be an 'oarie' boat, right enough. The oars are just in case. Now.

Everybody put on your life-jackets and we'll be off." He looked at the sky, noting the position of the sun. "We're all right for the next — oh — two to three hours, I'd say."

They watched him manoevre the boat round and away from the pier, away from the shore-rim where a few open boats and a green launch with a silver band were moored, away beyond the well-known, cone-shaped buoy that bobbed off-shore, until they were well and truly out at sea. It was then that Helen Stark, looking a bit worriedly at the water ahead, turned to Mr Ross and said, "What happens in two to three hours, sir? Why're we all right till then?"

Mr Ross laughed. "I just meant it'll be starting to get dark and we need to be off the water by then, unless someone's brought a torch."

Dick Baxter and Gardner said together, "I did."

"Ah — that would help a bit. Anyway, the best time to see a lighthouse is in the dark, isn't it?"

This question of falling darkness being both a problem and a desirable thing made everybody conscious of the quality of the light as the boat ploughed further and further out to sea. The air was getting much colder, and there was no doubt that the sun was going down in the sky, seeming to take with it a little cluster of cloud that gradually spread out below it. Mr Ross at the tiller scanned the sky constantly in between long gazes at the water ahead. In front of them, blocking the horizon, were the two large familiar islands of Narra and Buie to which steamers went back and forth every day.

"Is Morlie Bay on Narra, sir?" Dick asked.

"No. Eh — anyone know?" Mr Ross enquired. Nobody did. That, Betsy knew fine, suited him very well.

"Good. Good. Well, pay attention to the direction we'll take, for I'll be asking for a decent map from you later. Dick. Here! You take charge of this, will you? We should take readings every fifteen minutes or so."

From his pocket he handed to Dick, the crew's maths genius, a small compass, pad and pencil. "We should be heading South south-west until we're clear of the southern end of Narra, then we sail West, then North-west. How're we doing?"

Dick had been sitting gazing at the mountains of Narra with his hands deep in his parka pockets when Mr Ross broke into his thoughts. Betsy and the others exchanged looks at the sight of Dick's little struggles to get his hands free of his pocket linings which had come out with his hands as he reached for the compass. In spite of his awkward relations with his clothes, they knew Dick to be the best brain among them and the right one for the compass job.

Betsy wondered just what job Mr Ross would be likely to dish out to the rest of them in the course of the expedition. She looked round at her fellow sailors and asked herself if he would manage, as he'd done with Dick, to fit the job to the person quite so well.

Jack now, he would be the best one to do any kind of building that was required, like a shelter for the night. Robbie Stark, who admired Jack, would make a splendid, attentive helper. His sister Helen was a tidy wee soul. She'd be great at keeping everybody's belongings in their proper places. She was also a great flower-gatherer and often brought posies to school for the teacher's desk. Gardner? If Mr Ross had any sense, he'd delegate Gardner as the expedition's bird-recorder and wildlife spotter. Because of Gardner's natural bent for guardianship, he wouldn't need to be told to keep a general watch over safety matters, especially as regards wee Andy Kyle whose chief skill, as far as Betsy could tell, was speed! Perhaps that would come in handy too. Lena Drummond was a problem. Betsy only knew her as a great gossip, just like her mother. She loved telling about people — the more romantic the better. Maybe she could tell them stories, then, if they couldn't get to sleep or something. That left Betsy herself. There she drew a blank! What *she* was good at was seeing what *other folk* were good at! Anyway, like as not, she'd end up doing a bit of everything, the way it was at home. Maybe she could chip in with a poem after Lena's story.

The sky was changing colour all right, the reds of sundown beginning to fill the western half. The boat rounded the southern tip of Narra. Mr Ross pointed to a tiny island off shore which proved to have a family of seals playing on its rocks.

"They can change to folk," said Lena, thrilled by the old stories.

"How?" Jack wanted to know.

"Silkies. Seal men. They can change to people and come on land and live among us and we never know and they go back to the sea whenever they feel like it and just disappear."

Everybody had a longer look at the seals then. Maybe their heads were nodding, right enough? Soon Dick was telling Mr Ross to change direction for North-west. Clear of Narra, the wind was stronger, an Atlantic wind, and the sea seemed choppier. Mr Ross, perhaps with a view to keeping Helen Stark's apprehensions at bay, began to sing softly.

> Speed, bonnie boat, like a bird on the wing.
> Onward! a sailor's cry.
> Carry the lad that's born to be king
> Over the sea to Skye.

Then, without being invited, probably infected by the romance of the Skye Boat Song and the wonderful sunset, Lena Drummond sang too, in a special posh voice no one knew she had.

> If I were a blackbird I'd whistle and sing,
> And follow the ship that my true love sailed in,
> And in the top rigging I'd there build my nest,
> And pillow my head on her lily-white breast.

I'm only a young sailor, my story is sad.
I once was a gallant and brave sailor lad.
I courted a lassie by night and by day,
But now she has left me and gone far away.

And—if I were a blackbird I'd whistle and sing,
And follow the ship that my true love sailed in,
And in the top rigging I'd there build my nest,
And pillow my head on ... her ... lily ... white ... breast.

She sang the last four words as a series of rising notes, the way singers did on the wireless. Then she turned to the others and grinned, giving Robbie Stark and Jack leave to whistle like blackbirds and follow the whistles with their version of bird-snores on the lady's breast. Still, despite their romance-breaking nonsense, it had been a rather beautiful song.

"Where'd you learn that one, Lena?" Mr Ross asked, leaning back comfortably by the tiller.

"My Granda," she answered.

"Oh yes," Mr Ross went on, "Grannies and Grandas often know the best songs — old songs — many not even written down, just passed on, changed a bit, added to maybe."

"My wee sister Nan made my mother make up a bit of a song," Betsy put in. "She was singing that one about the woman that loses her baby when she goes gathering blaeberries. You know."

"*I* don't," said Jack. Robbie nudged him gently. "Sassenach," he whispered.

"How's it go?" Jack insisted.
"You do it with me, Lena."

> I left my baby lying here, lying here, a-lying here,
> I left my baby lying here,
> And went to gather blaeberries
>
>> Hovin hovin gorio-go, gorio-go, gorio-go
>> Hovin hovin gorio-go
>> I've lost my darling baby-o.
>
> I saw the swan upon the lake, upon the lake, upon the lake,
> I saw the swan upon the lake
> But nowhere saw my baby-o.

"She then traces the otter to his lair, and the fox to his den, I think, but never finds her baby. Anyway, Wee Nan couldn't thole that and my mother had to make up a verse that told how the woman *did* find her baby."

"And where did she?" asked Lena, her eyes shining.

"I think it was *I saw the shepherd and his dog and then we found my baby-o*, the idea being that the daft woman had strayed too far from the place where she'd left her baby and it was there the whole time."

"You'd think," said Dick, ever reasonable, "that she'd have heard it crying and found it that way."

"Ah!" said Mr Ross, having listened to their conversation without a word so far. "But songs and stories don't depend on the logic of the real world. A bit of mystery is the traditional mark of old songs and ballads, you know. They often leave you to guess."

Suddenly, as they looked at Mr Ross, a flash of light crossed his face and continued past him across the water at his back. It was eerie. They gazed about them and when the flash came again they saw where it came from.

"It's the lighthouse!"

"The light must've just gone on."

"It's still a good way off, isn't it?"

"Sir? How far now? I'm starving!" That was Andy Kyle.

Mr Ross looked at him cheerfully. "Then you'll eat a hearty supper, Andy. Not long now."

The boat's progress seemed to be hampered by the rougher waves out here, so that the island seemed to stay at a steady distance from them. But at last they saw the lighthouse itself raised on a dark hill above a pale curve of bay into whose quiet water the boat at last sailed. They were all stiff from sitting and eager to stretch their legs along that lovely curve of sand. But before she could follow the others in a spot of walking acquaintance with land, Betsy was beckoned by Mr Ross as he made the boat secure on the beach.

"A word with you, Betsy. It's about dividing the work among all of you. I think you're a decent judge of who might be best suited to what. So what do you think?"

She was astonished for a moment that something she'd already given her mind to should so soon afterwards be asked of her. She told Mr Ross what she thought and when the others were called together again, Mr Ross explained about jobs.

"We'll need a fire built somewhere close in to the cliff, Jack. You can arrange that, with Robbie's help. Everyone can gather firewood while we've still got some light. Right? Now Dick, since you've started with the compass and such, will you take charge of the map-making tomorrow? Gardner? You've no doubt noted already the sea birds *en route*. You can record the ornithological inhabitants of the isle tomorrow. Helen, would you mind being our conservation watch — make sure we don't leave any rubbish about and see that everybody tidies up properly after meals. We need a botanist, too, so you could help in that department. Lena, you be our diarist, recording the events from the time we left the pier, including weather and other natural phenomena. Andy, you could help Dick with his distance gauging for the map, for you'll be needing to go right round the isle to do it properly.

"Now, is everybody happy with their jobs? You can swap about, if you like. No? There you are, then, Betsy. That shows *you've* done *your* job well, as Personnel Adviser first of all. Now I'm going to ask *them* what they think you could do for some other job."

He raised his eyebrows enquiringly at the others. "Well? What else could Betsy do?"

There was complete silence. Just like the thing, Betsy thought. There's nothing special about me. Then Jack said something to Gardner who nodded.

"Sir?" Jack said. "She could tell us a story before we go to sleep, maybe a ghost story. She reads lots of stories and poems, Gardner says."

"Excellent!" Mr Ross clasped his hands together with a smack. "So we're all set. Any questions?"

"What's the name of this island?" Dick asked. "Did you tell us before?"

"No, I didn't. I wondered when you'd ask. It's Skellen Isle."

They all looked about, taking in the various characteristics of the place as far as they could see, and murmured the name. Skellen Isle. Betsy thought it had a familiar echo to it. She peered up at the lighthouse on the hill above. That was it! That poem, *Flannen Isle!* Talk about a mystery! She wondered if she could remember the whole of it and, if she could, would that be a rare camp story to go to sleep on? Maybe it would be too scary, at that. She'd better think of another.

All the same, she kept thinking about the eerie story of that other lonely lighthouse, manned by three men. When their relief had arrived one time, they'd found no trace of the three, although the table was set for a meal, the kettle still hot on the hob, the food still warm on the plates. The mystery was never solved. Three black sea-birds had been seen on a sea-wave, though. She shivered.

Jack and Robbie soon had a fire going on which to warm some soup. Mr Ross produced a large packet and water from a gallon container. The resulting brew was delicious. They sat round, drinking from their tea-mugs, starting on their first lot of sandwiches. The lighthouse beam swept out over the sky and the water from time to time. It was a quick meal, they'd all been so hungry, which suited the pace they needed to beat the on-coming dark. Mr Ross sent them off in two directions, the girls one way, the boys another, "to answer any calls of nature".

"Right, now. We'll away up to the lighthouse. All got your bags?" Mr Ross called, gathering them together from their stravaiging along the shore. "I'm leaving you to find the best way up, of course, seeing I've forgotten it myself!"

As it turned out, there was no one best way for everybody. For Andy Kyle the best way was the steepest and shortest. For Jack it was a ridge that offered footholds discoverd by himself. Dick disappeared from sight and unaccountably reappeared shortly at the top. Gardner, with his long legs, found a way where he only needed half a dozen climbing strides using some humps of rock. Robbie and Helen took the same route together by means of a little gulley with grassy clumps to hold on to.

After cautiously watching the others to the top, Lena chose the way of Robbie and Helen. Betsy, still absorbed in that old mystery, found that she'd climbed the rocks without thinking, merely following her nose, and it was only when she was nearly at the top that she realised she was climbing straight and easy — on steps! Joining the others on the hill, she looked back and saw a fairly regular series of steps cut in the rock a few feet to the right of the place where she'd started to climb. None of them had seen it in the fading light, and *she'd* only stumbled on it by chance!

Mr Ross was still on the shore below, waiting, and they knew what he was waiting for. The long, flashing arm of the lighthouse beam reached across the dark water behind him. They discussed the matter.

"He knew those steps were there all the time, I bet!"

"Aye, but he'd forgotten where they were. He *says*!"

"Never even mentioned them!"

"Steps are *easy*. Maybe he wanted us to practise Injun Joe Knew It, eh?"

"*What?*"

"He means *ingenuity*."

"Here! Let him find the steps himself. *He* made *us*."

"Aye. No telling!"

They peered down at Mr Ross who cupped his hands round his mouth and called up "Well done! Who found the steps?"

They all pointed to Betsy to indicate that the steps *had* been found.

"Where are they?" shouted Mr Ross.

They gave a huge collective shrug and Gardner struck his forehead to show sudden and total loss of memory while the others stood shaking their heads dumbly.

Mr Ross dropped his hands slowly and for a moment he stood still in the fast fading evening light. Then he threw his head back and gave a shout of laughter, turned right round and laughed out to sea. They could hear him fairly pealing it out. Then he looked back up at them and shouted one thing. "Touche! You got me!"

"What's he say?" asked Robbie.

Mr Ross had managed to find the steps and mounted quickly, reaching the others with a mockglower in greeting. He put his hands on his waist, panting, then grinned at them. "To the lighthouse," he said softly and began to walk up the grassy hill to the little dyke that ringed the base of the whitewashed lighthouse. They fell in behind him.

Passing through the white-painted gate, Mr Ross mounted some steps to the heavy door. The others stood round him, watching, as he lifted his hand to knock. At his touch, the door swung open. "He's left it open for us. Up we go."

It was a narrow winding stairway they had to follow now, lit by some high-placed light above.

"Hello, the house!" called Mr Ross. "We've arrived, John!"

The only sound was their footsteps on the stone

stairs and the echo of Mr Ross's voice ringing round the rough wall.

"Are you asleep on the job, John man?" Mr Ross called again. Still no answer came.

"Hey," Gardner whispered to Betsy, "Flannen Isle, eh?"

She flashed him a look and a shush, but she'd had the same prickly thought. For a moment she wondered if Mr Ross had planned *this*, but he seemed genuinely puzzled by the apparent absence of the lighthouse-keeper, John Livingstone, at this time of night.

They at last stepped into a room at the top. Somewhere in the background was a humming, pumping sound. "What's that noise?" asked Helen.

"Must be the generator, for the light," explained Mr Ross. They looked round the room.

"Look. The table's set."

"And the kettle's got a bit of steam coming from its spout."

"He can't be far away, then."

"Well, where is he?"

They all looked at each other and then at Mr Ross who was frowning thoughtfully. Then all at once they heard the heavy door downstairs being closed with a thud and the sound of a single pair of feet tramping up the steps. The tramping kept halting and a voice kept saying something, yet everyone knew that John Livingstone kept the Morlie Bay lighthouse on his own. He liked being alone, Mr

Ross had told them ages ago, and when the authorities had broached the plan of making the lighthouse automatic, John had made a special request to be left in charge, even if it meant paying him less. Could the solitude have become too much for him? Had he created, as some children do, an imaginary friend with whom to talk as he went about his business?

They waited wordlessly, listening to the footsteps coming nearer, the voice now clearly saying, "That was a fine walk for ye, eh? Nae muckle exercise for ye here, lad, but never mind. An' now for a bit o' meat for ye an' me." This was followed by a heavy sigh, just as the man himself pushed open the door of the little room where the children and their teacher stood.

John Livingstone came in. He was a big man in blue jeans and an Aran jumper, with a full red beard. He gave a start of surprise and pleasure at the sight of his visitors, and his hearty greeting was far from the tone of a melancholy man.

"Aha! So ye've managed it, eh? Well, ye're a sight for sore eyes. I've just been for a dander wi' . . ."

As he turned in the doorway, a shadow by his feet moved into the room, wagging its tail, sniffing round the feet of the children. Betsy and Gardner stared in astonishment, disbelief and recognition all at once.

"That's Young Laird!"

"It's Laird! It's our Dad's dog."

Their smell had been a start, but the sound of

their voices calling his named confirmed Young Laird's own recognition of *them*. He came to Gardner, folding his ears and ducking his head — the familiar dog-gesture of coming under the invisible canopy of a kindly master — and quietly sat by his feet.

7
Behind the Old Door

If Betsy and Gardner were surprised at the finding of Young Laird, John Livingstone was even more amazed at their story of how he'd come to be lost in the first place.

"There's devilment afoot, I'd say," he proclaimed. "Stealin' a man's dog like that is bad enough, when it's for money. But doin' it just to take it out in a boat an' droon the poor beast, that's devilment!"

"Yes," murmured Mr Ross, sitting at the table and watching the way Young Laird pressed close to Gardner's leg. "Whoever it was knew sheepdogs well enough to know they can be removed many miles overland from home and still find their way back if they get loose. It's peculiar they'd have taken him so far out to sea if all they wanted to do was drown him. There's plenty of water between the mainland and Narra for that."

"Maybe," Betsy suggested, deeply troubled by unknown motives for such cruelty, "it wasn't supposed to happen like that at all. Maybe they just took him out when they went fishing or something and he got away and swam to Morlie Bay."

"He certainly swam, a'right," said John

Livingstone. "I saw him mysel' crawlin' up o'er the rocks like a drookit rat. At exhaustion's door, he was, just ten days ago."

Everybody looked at Young Laird, healthy and sleek now. John said he'd keep him there for the time being till Gardner was ready to go home.

Andy Kyle yawned in the tired silence that had fallen on them.

"Right, John, show us the light deck." Mr Ross got up smartly. "I think we've enough energy left for that before we retire to our sleeping quarters for the night."

"Do we have far to walk to that cave of yours, sir?" Robbie wanted to know. "You said we'd camp in the cave."

"Don't be daft," said Andy. "It's full of water — a *sea*-cave."

"I don't care. He *said* we'd camp in it." Robbie looked sulky.

"Robbie. Andy. You're both right. And it's not far. You'll see," said Mr Ross soothingly. "After we have a look at John's workroom."

Betsy and Jack exchanged looks. "It's pitch dark now," she whispered. "Can you see us looking for some cave now? With just two torches?"

"All part of the exercise," he whispered back.

They filed through a narrow doorway behind the others. This led to a small flight of steps up to the light deck. Looking out over the sea, they could see in the light of the beam the water moving below, breaking in short rough waves on the rocks at each curved end of the bay. The tide must have come far in, for the pale expanse of sand had narrowed considerably and the moored motor boat looked to be well afloat.

"Now, then, Dick. Compass ready?" said Mr Ross solemnly.

Following Mr Ross's directions, Dick led the group downstairs until they fetched up against the shadowy wall at the bottom. Now they could see the narrow door in it.

Made of some kind of heavy, weathered wood encrusted over with tiny barnacles, against the wall it had been somewhat camouflaged.

Dick stepped forward and sought for a handle but found that the door pushed open on a strong spring. Beyond the door, in the light of Gardner's torch, could be seen the beginning of yet another flight of uneven steps downwards. Also, there was a cold, seaweedy smell and a hollow sound coming from below.

"Do we have to go down there, sir?" asked Andy Kyle in a scared voice. "It's awful dark-like, is it no?"

Mr Ross called back up the stairs to John Livingstone that they were ready for the lights now. In a moment, the darkness beyond the old door was a blaze of light, inviting and safe. Mr Ross went first now — just to check on certain things, he said, like crumbly stairs and stray spiders' webs. He said this with a certain tone that mocked any fear of such things and still gave him an excuse to precede them reassuringly into the unknown.

"This must be his road to the cave he talked about," whispered Lena, taking Helen's hand.

Betsy was feeling bone weary and not inclined to any further revelations this night. She was glad when Mr Ross's voice ahead said brightly, "And *here* . . . we are!"

"No before time," muttered Robbie, sitting down on the step he was on.

It was the cave, all right, very large and high-roofed, with a single cable of lights flung across the space from rocky wall to rocky wall. They were well clear of the water that was covering the floor of the cave at present. It provided just enough depth to float what was, at long last, Mr Ross's famous boat. She was moored by taut ropes to two heavy hooks driven into each of the cave walls. Higher still were more hooks of an even sturdier quality.

They gazed in silence. The boat was blue and white, long and low, with a row of four small round windows just along the water line. In small, neat letters written along the side was *Bird on the Wing*. She rocked gently below them as, every little while, a wave breaking far outside sent in a new swell.

"Hold on a minute, now," said Mr Ross. He reached above their heads and slid from a long natural shelf above the light cable a thick plank with narrow strips of wood nailed across it at intervals not unlike the ramp at Mowdy Mains to allow the hens up into the loft in the old barn to lay.

Mr Ross manoevred the plank, with help from Jack and Dick, into position.

"We'll now walk the plank. When over, go down that wee stair and through that wee door and you'll be below. Wait for me there. Right, who's first? Come on, Jack."

Mr Ross made the crossing in two steady strides. Reaching back, he offered a helping hand to them as, one by one, they followed suit. Some accepted his hand gratefully, while others pretended not to notice it out of personal pride in their powers of balance and a steady foot.

Soon they were gathered "below" in the shadowy interior of the boat. Mr Ross lit a lamp and again they had their eyes filled with yet another new sight.

"Are we going to sleep here, then, sir? In . . . *those*?"

"Yes. That's the idea, anyway. What d'you think?"

"*Drake he's in his hammock an' a million miles away,*" quoted Jack, clearly taken with the look of the two sets of hammocks slung up in vertical pairs, four on each side of the small apartment, with a bar above the top ones, presumably for heaving oneself up and in.

"You can decide among yourselves who'll be up and who down. I'm away to make us some cocoa —

just dried milk, mind, but it'll be good for us. Then you'll sleep, and so will I. Helen, come and help. Gardner, will you look out the sleeping bags — under yon cupboard in that big drawer there's three. The rest are rolled up in that chest by the door. Through here is the kitchenette and the galley and the dining-room, all in one, see."

Andy Kyle looked anxiously at their shelter for the night. "Sir? What if . . .?" he began and stopped.

"And," went on Mr Ross, "the toilet facilities, being modest themselves, are modestly placed away at the stern yonder. A torch will be kept handy for night visits, if need be. Eh — while you're waiting for the cocoa, you can practise getting into bed. There's a knack to it."

He was right. It was only when they were at last settled that Betsy, who was sure holding her breath had been the answer, asked, "How did *you* do it, Jack? I held my breath."

The others presented *their* methods.

"I put one leg in flat and hitched my whole body in."

"I held onto that bar with my ankles and hands — like a sloth — and then just dropped in."

"Well, I went in face down and turned with care."

"Help! I'm *still* face down. Turn with care, did you say?"

"I just held that bar and gave a bit hop up is all."

"I don't *know* how I did it. Well, we're in, anyway."

Mr Ross came through from the kitchen with a tray of mugs. Helen came behind with a plate of tea biscuits. Mr Ross stopped and looked at the smugly occupied hammocks. "Well done! Course you'll have to get out and do it over again with the sleeping bags unzipped, lining the hammocks, and then get yourselves back the way you are and zipped up."

There was a series of groans followed by a variety of falling noises as the orderly leaving of a hammock proved to be as awkward as getting in, especially as the boat now seemed to be rocking more under their feet.

"What if we get sea-sick?" Lena wondered, sipping from her mug and then looking at it peculiarly.

"You don't get sea-sick in a hammock, Lena," Dick told her. "No matter which way the vessel rocks, the hammock hangs straight down, with gravity."

"Oh, that's fine, then," she said, sipping with renewed relish.

A short time later, successfully cocooned in their several sleeping bags, they lay silently waiting for sleep. Mr Ross produced a thin mat and his own sleeping bag which he laid out on the floor. Then he blew out the oil lamp and they could hear him zipping himself into the bag.

"Now", he said in a low voice into the darkness, for the cave's lights were now extinguished too, "how about a story, Betsy? Everybody listening?"

Betsy thought for a moment. "Would you like a

ghostie one?" she asked. "A mystery, like?" There was silence in all hammocks.

"I could tell a really good love story," said Lena helpfully.

"Ghost story! Quick! Mystery!" was the alarmed chorus.

So Betsy, summoning her recitative skills, gave them *Flannen Isle* in its entirety. Finally, she intoned the last dramatic lines.

> *Three men alive on Flannen Isle*
> *Who thought on three men dead.*

She told herself it wasn't *too* scary for them. Because they too had come into the Morlie Bay lighthouse and found it empty of its keeper that night, with the table set and the kettle boiled, just as in the poem, there was some first-hand identification with that experience. But because John Livingstone had shortly come clumping up the stairs alive, well, and very substantial, they could enjoy the chilly story from the comfort of their own happy ending.

"They got changed into yon big birds, I bet," said a voice. "Or *silkies*."

"Or maybe they went mad and jumped into the sea."

"And left their tea just like that? No, some emergency came up, more like."

"I don't think there's *any* mystery. They just got the meal ready for the *next* three and scarpered off home to the mainland in a helicopter. That's all."

"Well," said Dick's voice thoughtfully, "I've

heard of folk disappearing into thin air, only what happens is they fall into a time warp or something. It's quite complicated to explain. It's another dimension."

"De mention of which is too spooky for me," said Mr Ross. "What if it was just a dream the *poet* had? Eh? Dreams and old tales don't have to make ordinary sense, do they? I plump for a dream myself."

This interpretation seemed to be the signal for general drifting off to sleep. Just as she was dropping off, rocked pleasantly in her hanging bed, Betsy thought she heard Gardner muttering above her, "I wish the Young Laird affair was just a dream."

She'd been trying not to think about that one too much because of the weight of dread that it pressed on her heart. It was like carrying a stone there, hurting the other organs in her body. Coming on this excursion was a relief from all that. At least, now they had Young Laird to take home with them which would cheer their father, but the manner of the dog's appearance on Skellen Isle could only emphasise the fact that ill-will was coming from some direction to sour life at Mowdy Mains. These attacks on sheep and sheepdog were hitting at the very heart of a shepherd's life, she thought. Perhaps because she'd just been reeling off poetry and often thought in rhyme, anyway, she found herself thinking, half-asleep, "a shepherd's life, trouble and strife — that's rhyming slang for *wife* — *a shepherd's wife*."

She slept, her last thought of their mother.

8

A Long Day Learning

In the night, the *Bird on the Wing* rocked and pitched about as a sea squall came and passed. Although it seemed that they'd all been wakened now and again by the hollow thumping of waves hitting the sides of the boat, no one had been really alarmed, for the hammocks prevented any major tossing of bodies asleep.

What *did* alarm them was the position of the boat in the early hours of the morning. Jack discovered it first when he looked out of his porthole window.

"Hey! We're moving!" he cried.

"What d'you mean? We've been moving the whole night," answered Robbie. "Did you no feel it?"

"Yes, but this is moving *along*. We're sailing out to sea. Look!"

They all looked. They *were*.

"Where's Mr Ross?"

The place where he'd lain on the floor was bare, and there was no sign of his sleeping bag or anything. Betsy's mind flickered for a moment over the story she'd told them last night. Oh no! Not a mysterious disappearance in their very own midst!

Then she realised. "We're daft. Listen. The

engine's on. Mr Ross is taking the boat out, of course."

"Why?"

"Let's go and see."

On deck, they found Mr Ross at the wheel. He greeted them matter-of-factly. "So you're up at last. Right. There're the rods. Get fishing for breakfast."

He'd taken the *Bird on the Wing* well out and now he switched off the engine and dropped a small anchor overboard. Jack and Gardner, who had fished in Ballin Glen many a time, had soon baited and cast their hooks. Betsy showed Robbie and Andy how to do it and presently they too were at the ready. Then she baited Lena's hook for her, because Lena didn't like the touch of the grubs and, since there was just the one rod left, Betsy gave Helen first go of sharing it. Mr Ross had settled down on a corner of the deck by the wheel and pulled out a book, but she noticed that he was keeping watch occasionally over the top of its cover.

The sea was calm and glassy green-grey where they were. The sky was beginning to shed its morning mist. Skellen Isle in bright daylight, with its white lighthouse, green hill-top and dark ring of rocks broken by pale sandy bays, made Betsy think of the words "dreaming isle" that she'd read somewhere, or maybe made up herself. It looked like a new land, a little kingdom, a simple place with no problems to bother folk. And yet, even out here, it *had* been touched — by their problem.

In the still silence of fishers waiting for a bite, out of some deep, clear place in her mind that had given her her last thought before going to sleep the night before, was born an intuition. It was that the "devilment" being suffered at Mowdy Mains was aimed not at their father himself but *through* him at their mother!

With her eyes on the distant horizon where the sea-mist lay in a last band, Betsy thought around this idea. Hadn't she noticed how their father had looked at their mother once in a funny, alarmed way? When *was* that look? And what about her crying in the byre that time? She'd heard their father saying, "I know it's no your fault" or something. She tried to remember that look again, and Wee Nan came to mind. Wee Nan. Nan telling them at the table how she and Betsy had met Mr Weaver at the Sea Serpent and he'd asked kindly after their mother's hens. *That's* when the funny look was exchanged. So.

"That man", their mother had called him, wishing they'd never relied on him for something.

Ty Weaver, Betsy said to herself, remembering his sheepskin waistcoat and how uneasy she'd felt in his presence. And suddenly, as she recalled his words, "Tell your mother I asked, mind." She knew it had been *seeming* kindly. But to say a kindly thing, and not mean it, and to ask the thing to be relayed — why, that was truly villainous. And the brief look of alarm it obviously aroused in their parents? That pointed to something more. Could Ty Weaver have been sending them some sort of threat?

"Why the big sigh, Betsy?" Mr Ross had been watching her, then, over his book cover.

"Oh — just . . ." She shrugged.

"A sigh of contentment? Here on the blue ocean wave?"

"Aye."

"I see. Is that why you look so worried, eh?"

She was saved from further interrogation by a shout from Robbie. "I've got one! I've got one! What do I do now?"

The sea seemed to become full of fish as one by one each fisher landed a catch on the deck. The tempo of the day was set. It was industry, activity, tasks and projects from then on. First, having caught enough fish for their own breakfast and John Livingstone's, they took the *Bird on the Wing* right round the island for fun. They saw some incredible birds diving deep down into the clear water. "Gannets," said Gardner.

"That's what my mother calls us when we eat a lot," said Robbie, who was fascinated by the birds. He watched them particularly closely now. As they returned to the cave-mooring, he could be heard saying to himself, "Bloomin' marvellous, them gannets!"

Soon it was over the plank, up the tunnel, through the old door, up the stairs, onto John's table with the cleaned catch, then into the frying pan with it, and at last they tasted the delicious food, talking all the while.

"Hm. Fruits of our labours," murmured Betsy.

"Can you call fish fruits?" asked Lena.

"The French do. *Fruits de mer* they call sea food," Mr Ross said.

"*Fruits de mère*? That's fruits of the mother, isn't it?" Dick asked.

"Different *mer*. Though the sea *is* thought of as a mother, in myths and such. Out of the sea came all life, see."

"But," said Dick, putting an elbow on the table, shifting his fork to his other hand and waving it as he spoke, "what about the sun? Can't produce much without the sun and all that the sky does. I mean, the winds, the clouds . . ." He stopped talking, fork in air, as though he'd come up against some bigger idea that he'd no name for. It threw him off his eating stride. Those watching saw him go through the motions of having mislaid his fork and of finding it in his own hand.

"Well," said Mr Ross, "I can see we'll have to do something on the Universe soon. Questions are a good way to start. Keep your questions in mind. But for today, now, we've enough on our hands.

"John, we'll leave you now," said Mr Ross, when breakfast was finished, "but I think Gardner would like to take Young Laird with him while he goes birdwatching. Now, everybody listen for a moment while we recap on our projects. Now, we've come to an island, all right, but not a desert isle, not an uninhabited one. The inhabitant on this one, John here, is part of the island's character, if you like, and as such we can consider him one of its phenomena. You don't mind being a phenomenon, John? Well, that beard is, if you're not!"

John Livingstone laughed and scratched the phenomenon growing on his face. "Aye, on ye go, Doug."

"Well," continued Mr Ross, "Jack and Robbie, this is for you. You've seen how the lighthouse works at night. Now, there are three parts to your job. First, work out the dimensions and plan of the lighthouse on paper (for a model later), then interview John about the life he lives, and then I think he's got a special task for you lined up. Okay? A bit of anthroplogy, that. Right. Helen, I said we'd need a botanist. In other words, record the *flora* to be found. I've brought this for you. D'you know what it is?"

He handed her from his haversack what looked like a pile of wooden table mats held together with clamps. She shook her head, examining it.

"That's a flower press, isn't it?" Jack offered. "I made one of them once in a woodwork class I took somewhere."

"Right, Jack. You can show Helen how to use it. You *can* use a thick book, of course, to press them. Who volunteers to assist Helen? There's a writing part to this, too."

Betsy decided she'd like this job. "Good. Thank you, Betsy. Each specimen has to be identified. John has a book on his shelf to lend. And *I* like to see a description of the habitat of each one — what's growing near it, what the soil is like, in the shade or not, that kind of thing. Dick and Andy, you're the map-makers. That's clear. Gardner, birds for you. Lena? You and I will walk round the island and check how everyone's getting on. It would be interesting to note what problems might come up and how they're solved — or not. Also, we'll keep a weather watch. What d'you think, John? Is it going to stay fine like this?"

John squinted out of the window near him. "It could. But I've seen days that started fresh as a daisy endin' up wi' a cracker o' a thunderstorm."

"In that case, to work! Give us — oh, three hours should do it — till noon. Then a swim, food, and home across the water."

Cartographers, botanists, anthropologists, and solo ornithologist with dog set off about their jobs. Diarist and expedition leader stayed in the lighthouse to wash up the breakfast dishes, thereby giving the others some time to get going, and also to bring the diary up to date so far, there being a lot to cover already. Mr Ross had offered to assist Lena with this so that she wouldn't get *too* carried away with her own romantic thoughts, since it was to be a diary of the *whole* expedition. Lena had already been heard rapturising over their night on board as being "rocked in the cradle of the deep" which was, apparently, a line from another of her Granda's old songs.

By the end of the three hours, Betsy and Helen had collected some twenty different flowers, not all of them identified yet. Gardner had found several types of gulls, more bloomin' marvellous gannets, and even some meadow pippits among inland heathery hillocks. Dick and Andy had discovered another sea-cave on the other side of the island along with a tiny, lagoon-like cove. Jack and Robbie had helped John Livingstone to build a new hen-run for his six-member brood of leghorns hidden away among some whins, and Lena and Mr Ross had just noted in the diary that the sky to the South was gathering something ominous.

They were all very hot from their labours, so that the promised "dook" down by the motor-boat came as a wonderful relief. Even Young Laird overcame his previous surfeit of sea-water and splashed gratefully with the children. There were rumbles in the distance.

The storm broke very suddenly, sending them racing, dressing *en route*, for the shelter of the lighthouse. John Livingstone had switched off the generator and his electrical main, for he knew that lightning can search out such kindred energy sources and create a live, blue, frightening thing. Although the lighthouse had a sturdy lightning conductor fastened all down its outside wall, John wasn't inclined to trust it entirely.

Gathered round the table in John's living quarters, they ate the last of their sandwiches and fruit. John produced some small bottles of ginger ale from his stocks and proper beer for himself and Mr Ross.

"How will we get home, sir? With the storm, like?" Andy wanted to know. All faces turned to Mr Ross, eating abandoned for the moment. Clearly Andy was expressing a shared anxiety.

"We'll see. The worse it is, the sooner it'll be over — eh, John?"

John looked back at his friend seriously. "Maybe aye, and maybe hooch aye. I'll tell ye this much, I'll no be lettin' any boat away from here if *I* don't consider it safe. Even if ye *do* have the school in the mornin'. There y'are!"

Mr Ross turned to them. "You see? John's the boss in this matter."

Betsy and Gardner exchanged looks of relief. You couldn't always be sure that Mr Ross would put caution above adventure, and there were times when she thought having him in charge was just a bit of a strain. In fact, now that she thought about it, life itself was a bit of a strain when you realised that your elders and betters weren't as all-knowing and all-powerful as all that, not all *that* wise. She caught Mr Ross's eye and he winked at her. Could he have had an inkling of her doubt of his wisdom? Was that why he'd turned authority over to John? To reassure them all? She wondered if he was truly wise after all.

She felt better, thinking it, as the storm around them cracked and thundered.

"Does that cave ever get really filled up?" Jack asked John Livingstone.

"Very rarely. Why?"

"I was thinking if the *Bird on the Wing* could get smashed against the roof."

"Well, it's never happened yet. I keep a good lookout, though. But did ye no see the cleeks high up — the great big fellows up near the roof? They're for securing her right out of the water if need be — like the way the fishin' boats are hooked up for safety in Thurso harbour, I hear tell."

Jack made some notes on this information. Mr Ross proposed the others use the time likewise, organising their projects on paper in readiness for their entire presentation to the class the following week. John's kitchen table became a communal desk, his bookshelf a reference library, himself a mine of information for the next hour.

They became so engrossed in what they were doing that they hardly noticed the passing of the storm, the quietening of the sky, and the time come for them to leave the island.

"Aye," said John, surveying the sky, "you'll have a fair crossin' now. But don't go tarryin' much longer."

He came with them to the beach to wave them off. He gave Young Laird a special pat and fondle of the ears. "Look after that one," he said. "Mind, now."

Gardner nodded, his hand curled round the dog's collar, holding Young Laird close to his leg.

John stood watching the boat go. When they were well out to sea, they could still see him standing on the shore. Then he turned and walked along the edge of the sea. That image of him walking by himself along the shore, not returning right away to his lighthouse, was the loneliest picture. For a moment, Betsy almost wished he could have kept Young Laird for company. John should certainly have a dog of some description, anyway, she thought sadly. Something about him, perhaps his solitariness, reminded her of Jack. She looked at their friend now. Yes, she could imagine Jack as a lighthouse keeper someday. It wasn't unlike keeping a treehouse, sending out code signals across the glen, as Jack used to do.

She wondered if the way people were when young was a good guide to what they'd become when grown. The question was, what *made* them the way they were when young? Especially them that were . . . well, not too nice. She remembered watching their mother bathing and dressing Wee Nan as a baby and how her seven-year-old self had remarked that it was sad about robbers and murderers because they had once been little babies like Wee Nan and had had a mother who loved them the way Wee Nan was loved by *their* mother. Ah well, their mother had answered, it's probably because they *weren't* so loved that's been their trouble. And so

Betsy had been even more convinced that being bad was a sad thing. She asked herself what sad baddie might be behind the mischief at Mowdy Mains. Again, it was Ty Weaver that came into her head when she thought of that.

It was a funny thing, but she had an impression of being on the way to a solution when she thought of their troubles. Why was that? Being on Skellen Isle, away from the main scene, seemed to clear her thoughts in some way. Or perhaps she was just paying attention to the right thing. The right thoughts were coming to her out of the confused tangle, and Ty Weaver kept being at the centre of it all — Ty Weaver and their mother.

They were past Buie and Narra and the mainland was in sight. Gardner scanned the sunlit hills above the Firth. "I wonder if he gathered the lambs for marking," he murmured. Betsy hoped not, and that their mother's notion of a day off had prevailed. It was cloudless over those hills and perhaps had been all day, the sort of Sunday that brought people in groups out from the towns to walk in the surrounding hills and climb to the tops of the highest of them.

Soon she and Gardner and Jack, having taken leave of the others one by one as they passed through the village, were back on their own hill. As they breasted the top and the Mowdy Mains ground lay before them, they could see no flock gathered behind the farm, hear no bleating that went with a "handling". So it looked as though there had indeed been a day off.

"I wonder if they went anywhere. And where," Betsy remarked.

They'd be spotted, as all traversers of the hill were, as soon as their silhouettes appeared against the sky. Any moment now would come running Rannie, Jocky and Wee Nan to meet them.

"Yonder's some folk on horseback coming down the Pony Road, isn't it?" Gardner observed. He put his fieldglasses to his eyes. "Hey. It's the Castle bairns and . . . well, I'll be . . . There's another one. Come on."

As the two groups approached one another, astonishment grew in the one on foot. Look Slippy, mounted on their own horses, had Jocky and Wee Nan up in front of them. Rannie, a picture of pride, was astride a third steed, a sturdy little garron with shaggy hooves and rough coat.

"Whose is this one?" Jack asked, stroking its muzzle, waiting for an answer that didn't come right away.

When the answer did come, it was entirely perfect. All day the unnamed horse had accompanied the three Blair children, their parents, and Look Slippy, to Ballin Brae on a picnic to Flo Jinty's place. It was going to join Clover the cow in her pasture by the burn and be Jack's.

9

Pet Days

The return of Young Laird was greeted with such familial joy at Mowdy Mains as made everyone ready to believe that things might be "looking up". Whatever devilment had been causing trouble had perhaps been outwitted by some more kindly force. Laird's recovery felt to the Blairs like their own personal victory.

The summer began to give much heart to all concerned in a series of gladdening developments.

First of all, on the work side at Mowdy Mains, the two days of the clipping proved to be "scorchers", so that the weather for a change was with the men. As always, men came from neighbouring sheep farms to help with the handling. When Mowdy Mains was done they'd move round in turn to one another's farms and Ewan Blair would go with them. It was a time-honoured system that had been in use for generations, a kind of bartering of labour that got the job done and was at the same time a series of social occasions. News would be exchanged, notes on farm conditions compared, stories told, and jokes shared. The children on the farms helped to roll the fleeces and pack them into large wool bags, so that everyone was involved in the work.

For the women, handlings were an anxious time, for with so many mouths to feed three times in the day, with tea and scones to bring out mid-afternoon, they were kept on the go from dawn till dusk. There was always the question of whether the food would go round and, most important, whether it would be worthy of good remark.

This particular handling, the Blairs' mother had an offer of help from Elenore Stewart who had taken to the place from the first time she'd come there that spring. Their father at early breakfast that morning had remarked, "Oh aye? She comin', eh? I wonder if she knows *he's* comin' up, or if *he* does that *she* is?"

The Blairs listened on the edges of this parental talk. Who was *he*?

"What're you talkin' about, Dad?" Rannie asked boldly.

"Nothin' for nosey folk. Eat your breakfast. And mind you stay out of the road the day. No like last year."

Last year, Rannie had narrowly escaped being "brained" by one of the tups leaping up from its shearing position, its fleece shed and it mad to recover its freedom.

Wee Nan was lifting the edge of the oilcloth on the table, examining the wood underneath. "How can a table be sad?" she asked to herself. Nobody heard. More loudly, she went on, "Anyway, *we've* got a sad table. So does Mrs Rutherford. Hers is *really* sad."

The others looked at each other now. Here was

Nan not making sense again. That meant something. They questioned her.

"Sad? What d'you mean *sad*? Nan, what're you talking about?"

"How d'you know about Mrs Rutherford?"

She answered, "Davy Rutherford in my class said it."

Their mother was truly puzzled. "Mrs Rutherford always has a great spread at handlings. I never hear the end of it when your father's been over there. Steak an' kidney pies, mountains of pancakes, blackcurrant tarts, and I don't know what all. The whole countryside knows about Mrs Rutherford's table just *groanin'* wi' food and . . . oh!" She looked keenly at Wee Nan and suddenly started to laugh, grasping their father's arm.

Rannie picked it up first. "*Groanin'*. Wi' food!" he chuckled, then got down on all fours and did an imitation of an overloaded table creaking and swaying and finally collapsing on the floor. "Like that!"

Betsy could see that Nan understood now all right, but that she was uncertain about the funniness of her misunderstanding. Gardner came to her rescue.

"*Some* folk would find a groaning table a sad sight — like them that can't eat!" he said, winking at Nan.

"Well," their mother observed, her laughing stopped as suddenly as it had begun, "our table *this* handling is not going to be that sad. In fact, it'll be downright *merry*, if you ask me. We don't have the stuff to put out, now that we have to be so careful. Still, I can always do plenty of scones and there's fresh cream and butter and the raspberries are good in the garden this year. We'll no do badly. Who'll pick the rasps?"

The boys were needed to help with the gathering of the sheep. "Don't pick the lot," Rannie said as they went out. "Leave some for us another day. Hey! Look who's comin' down the Pony Road!"

"It's Jack!"

"Walking."

"Leading Desmond."

"He *said* he'd do this one of these days."

They gathered by the gate to watch the approach of Jack and the shaggy little garron, Desmond, so named after Jack's uncle who'd died the previous year. He was leading the horse slowly and carefully over the rutted track out of consideration for the rider in the saddle — Flo Jinty herself, brought at last out of her glen to Mowdy Mains.

At the gate they stopped, Jack grinning at the obvious spectacle he'd created, Flo Jinty looking ahead of them to where their mother stood in the doorway shielding her eyes against the sun.

"Now, Chack, you haf got me up here, make haste to get me down again. I hope I can still walk about, with my knees knocking so. He would haf me come today when you are going to be so busy, but I can peel a potato, you know, Issabel."

"Over here," their father laughed, indicating the stile at the side of the gate. Jack manoevred Desmond so that Flo Jinty could step easily onto the top plank of the stile and, with a hand from Ewan Blair, stand on firm ground again. She turned to look at the Firth glittering in the haze. "It iss a long time since I haf seen the sea. Chack iss right. I should haf come here long ago, it iss so good to see it again, after all."

Betsy wondered what she meant by "after all", but Flo Jinty was moving towards their mother, holding out her hands and being taken indoors.

The next arrivals were Matt Fleming and Geordie Rutherford with two men each. And soon came Look Slippy on Carlos and Carmen who joined Desmond for the day in the Four Acre, a field away. Coming along a few minutes behind, wearing a bright blue, full-skirted dress and white sandals, her hair tied back on her neck with a blue ribbon, was Elenore Stewart. She walked with one arm by her side, the other hand on her hip, a style that seemed to balance the slight limp of her walk.

As the boys moved off to the hill with their father to gather in the flock from the lower hill to which they'd been herded from the remotest parts the day before, half of Look Slippy went with them, the other half joining Nan among the raspberries. It was the first time this had ever happened. That was another thing to be glad about, probably, though Betsy wondered how they would manage to speak, separated like this, considering the dependence on one another to finish a sentence. Perhaps it was even possible they wouldn't be able to *think* at all, never mind talk, unless they were together.

She was so engrossed in the phenomenon of Look Slippy split up that she almost missed the moment when Elenore Stewart, just paces away, stopped and turned to look at the view that included the winding path over the hill to the village down which at that minute was striding a figure. When Elenore turned back, it seemed to Betsy that she smiled with her mouth in a secret sort of way. Even when she greeted Betsy, the secret stayed smiling in her eyes.

"Hello, Betsy. I hear you had a grand excursion to Skellen Isle and collected some of its flora. Can I see them some time?"

"Yes. But Mr Ross has the album now. For reference in the school library."

"Mr Ross, is it? Well, I must ask *him*, then. I'll do that." She sighed. "The next time I see him."

Betsy looked at her, then past her at the hill path. "Here he is now, coming here." She recalled the exchange between their parents at breakfast. "Must be to help with the clipping."

Elenore followed Betsy's look. "Yes. It must be for the clipping, right enough." But she still had that secret look. Betsy knew then who the *he* and *she* were that their father had meant. Now, too, she knew *what* he had meant that "nosey folk" shouldn't ask about. Well, she thought, if they want a budding courtship to stay secret, a handling is the worst place to gaze at each other! And they'd better not let that romance-struck Lena Drummond get wind of it. That one'd soon have the whole bairn population in the district on the look-out for them at well-known trysting places as well as at those of her own invention.

It wasn't a question of spying on them, to catch them "canoodling", as it was called, but merely to accumulate sightings that would confirm a pending betrothal, so that folk could say, "Well, we all knew *months* ago!" Sometimes, if a courtship went on too long without any special announcements, folk had been known to bring up the matter at some gathering, saying outright, "An' when's the weddin' to be?"

She wondered if she ought to warn Elenore and Mr Ross about the way bairns spot and tell and how their parents can nudge and hint relentlessly about naming days before sweethearts themselves are ready for it. She wondered why it was that so many adults in the world reserved their heaviest teasing for growing children and young sweethearts — those going through vulnerabilities, in fact. Maybe it was a way of hardening them where they were soft, like sending the wee laddies to school in wintertime in short trousers "to toughen them up".

Anyway, Mr Ross and Elenore Stewart weren't young. They must be at least twenty-six or seven, well able to take on that kind of harassment. She was glad about them, mind, for she liked them.

"Have you noticed, Betsy?" Elenore was saying.

"Luke and Lippi have left one another? Moved apart?"

"Yes. I was wondering if they'll be able to talk, separately."

Elenore laughed, leaning on the gate, watching Mr Ross draw nearer. "It'll be interesting to see how they manage. That kind of togetherness . . ." But she didn't finish, for Mr Ross had her attention now in greeting. Betsy drifted away in to the kitchen where Flo Jinty was indeed sitting at the table helping to peel potatoes over a basin of water.

Betsy hovered by them for a few moments. There was something she'd been wanting to ask their mother for some time. Every so often she thought of it, but wasn't sure how best to tackle the thing. The trouble was that ever since the return from Skellen Isle, things had seemed so normal that Betsy had had her doubts. She wondered how far the favourable atmosphere could be trusted. Perhaps it was like pet days.

A "pet day" was what their father called a balmy, mild day following a stretch of fierce weather. It wasn't expected to last and usually didn't, the fierce weather resuming right away. A pet day, he said, was the weather sucking up to folk — all very nice, a day to remark on for its beauty, a wee gift of a day, to say sorry.

What Betsy wondered was whether, after the bad weather of their fortunes before Skellen Isle, this lovely summer was just a kind of extended pet day.

Maybe they should be prepared for more rough days beyond.

It *was* a lovely summer, too. At the clipping the men remarked on the "good rise" the sheep had which made their job easier, the "rise" being the new wool growing already below the fleece that's to be clipped, leaving a perfect cutting line to follow. Eighteen enormous wool bags were filled with fleeces and collected by the wool-growers from Glasgow. Ewan Blair marked in his own personal little green book the favourable prices quoted to be paid to Sir Guy for the wool.

The dipping that followed shortly was accomplished during warm days with a breeze blowing from the sea so that neither animals nor men became too hot. Only one ewe was found infested with the dreaded maggots, the patch treated with straight dip. The men remarked that the young Mowdy Mains lambs this year looked to be the best in the district and would likely top the market come September-October and more than make up for the losses of that spring when the worrying had happened.

The Blairs spent a good part of the holidays on three projects that came about as a result of Mr Ross seeming to be almost daily in the offing. Projects were inevitable with him in the picture.

"Ewan," the Blairs heard him say to their father one day, "what's to happen with all those beeches that were blown down up by?"

"I'd like to see the lot made into logs for the winter, myself. But they're no my trees, you see. It's up to Sir Guy."

The way their father talked about storing *anything* for the winter, you'd have thought he'd forgotten they wouldn't be here then.

"Would you like me to have a word with him?" asked Elenore Stewart who seemed always to be around whenever Mr Ross was around.

Their father frowned. "If you do it for yourselves, that's fine wi' me. But I'm leery o' anything on the side, like. I've been told I could have this or that for my beasts — through somebody else, like — and then I found out Sir Guy wasn't party to the arrangement, knew nothing at all about it."

Mr Ross and Elenore exchanged looks. So did the Blairs' mother and father. Betsy looked at Gardner who was frowning. She hadn't talked to him or anyone about the thoughts that had come to her on Skellen Isle to do with Ty Weaver, but Gardner had asked their father during the clipping why the grieve hadn't come to Mowdy Main. Their father had made some reply to the effect that it was only those with sheep to be clipped in return that needed to come and help him, besides which yon grieve wasn't fit to work at Mowdy Mains. Betsy had a good idea that by "fit" he had meant "suitable".

Also, there was the matter of the hayfield. Normally, when the folk at Mowdy Mains wanted a field sown, a tractor and seeder were sent up from the Howe. Later, in August or July, a reaper would arrive and then a baler. This year, wanting nothing to do with the Howe, Ewan Blair had reverted to an old traditional method of sowing. Although he'd managed to get his one field ploughed and harrowed by the Rutherford equipment from Ballin Farm, he'd decided to be as self-sufficient as possible after that. So, using an old sowing sheet that had been in one of the outbuildings for years, he'd strode up and down the field one long windless day in May, rhythmically sowing by hand. Now he had sharpened his scythe and was preparing to reap the hay himself, fork it in the sun, and build ricks and stacks with the help of his wife and children. Mr Ross, of course, had offered to help with the scything.

A few days later Elenore came up to Mowdy Mains with Look Slippy and brought news that Sir Guy would be only too pleased to have the fallen beech trees tidied off the hill. He'd send a forester up with a chain-saw to do the heavy cutting. He suggested bagging some logs for distribution to the old people in the district, if there was plenty.

So there was the log project and the hay-making to fill many days. When these tasks were done, Mr Ross thought of something restful but still constructive. This was blaeberry gathering.

No stravaigings over the hills in summer were without pauses and driftings off to eat the berries that grew in the heather, sometimes profusely, sometimes sparsely. The Blairs by now knew where the best clumps were, in which little glens, by which tiny burns. There was something about blaeberry picking that they liked better than stripping raspberry canes or plundering bramble bushes. Blaeberries were in the nature of a real find. The best would be found unexpectedly, by lifting the outside edges of an apparently barren clump or by parting to its heart a large bunch of heather. In the minds of blaeberry pickers runs always the thought, *I wonder*. And there is always the image of a little dark blue, misted, ring-topped berry leading them further afield. No wonder that the berry-gathering mother in the old song thus lost her darling baby-o!

Once, in typical hair-raising fashion, Rannie had followed *his* luck to the very brink of an overhanging brow of the deep gorge at the Martin Glen and narrowly missed pitching over. Gardner had seen where Rannie was heading and had luckily been on hand to grab his brother's ankle. This had merely served to give Rannie an idea and he'd urged Gardner to hold on just so while he reached for "thae beauties" growing below the cliff edge. But Gardner had said "damn the fears" and that the birds were welcome to them!

The Blairs' mother loved blaeberry picking even more than they did, it being that pleasing combination of rest and purpose. It reminded her of her childhood, too, as few things did at Mowdy Mains, for she'd been raised not among farming folk but in a small town in Fife where the children there used to take to the hills round about when the blaeberries were out.

Betsy came to empty her filled cup of berries into the main basket in their mother's custody. They were alone on the wide sweep of the hill under an empty sky. At that moment, Betsy had a sudden feeling that she could ask their mother anything and in return their mother could tell her anything.

"Mum? Does Weaver the Grieve not like you for some reason?"

What happened then could have been a mis-step as she turned, but their mother staggered and sat down swiftly, holding the basket away from her to keep it from spilling about her. She looked at her alarming daughter.

"What in heaven's name makes you ask that?"

Betsy wasn't to be put off. She couldn't explain, anyway. "Just tell me the truth. Please? You can tell me."

And so their mother told Betsy the truth. At the end of the telling, Betsy nodded to herself. It all fitted now, of course.

The soft wind played about her hair. The grass was warm on their bare feet. Isa Blair was looking inward at herself, as a girl far away from here.

Betsy thought of crabbit days and pet days and wondered what sort of days were ahead now.

10
Death in the Haggs

Far out on the hill, almost to the Back of the World, lay a section called the Haggs, much to be feared by man and beast. They were the worst sort of peat bog, black pools of mire that could suck down into their depths forever any living thing heavier than a wild bird. Sometimes, the surface would harden and dry and *look* stable enough. Sometimes they would be covered thickly over with a pale green weed that also *looked* substantial. But sheep and their shepherds and skilled hill walkers knew the deception of such surfaces and didn't go near them. The Blairs had a healthy horror of the Haggs.

One Sunday in August, berry gathering at an end, haying and logging completed, the Blairs set off to take Flo Jinty some of the jam that their mother had made from the blaeberries. She'd had quite a lot of raspberry jam, too, and Mr Ross had suggested selling a jar or two in the village. This had been a timely idea, for with the money from this she had got him to purchase for her a bag of corn for the hens. He himself and Elenore Stewart began to buy eggs from her every week, and that too was a help.

The day was breezy and cool with occasional hot rays from the sun when it came from behind piling clouds. The Blairs followed the Pony Road for some way before striking out for Ballin Brae.

Betsy recalled something she'd forgotten about Jack.

"Gardner? D'you mind seeing Jack bringing some planks up the glen? That day we took Look Slippy over to see him for the first time? Ages ago?"

"The day I saw the heron. Aye. Why?"

"I meant to ask him what they were for."

"Probably to build something — something for Flo Jinty or a shed for Clover, maybe."

"No. She has one, mind? Behind the cottage."

"Well, I don't know. Ask him the day."

Rannie and Jocky, ahead as usual, disappeared over a dip, followed by Wee Nan. Soon she reappeared, waving, waiting for Betsy and Gardner to reach her.

"Come and see!" she cried.

In a moment, out of the dip, came Rannie and Jocky walking backwards, as came Jack likewise, pulling the reins of Desmond to encourage him up the slope. He was in need of encouragement because he was, they now saw, harnessed to a small cart and was toiling at getting it up the incline. But he managed it, and Jack turned to his friends proudly. "Flo Jinty can ride in this, too, I reckon, when it's properly cleaned up and painted and I've put a seat in."

Betsy looked at Gardner. "There's my answer! Where'd you get the wheels, Jack?"

"Be careful, Rannie. Don't get behind it," Jack

cautioned his friend. "The wheels? They've been lying in Geordie Rutherford's old cart shed for years. He gave them to me."

"And the wood? Those planks you were carrying up the glen yon day?"

"Yes, well, they were left over from the time my Uncle Des built the cabin for himself. Perfectly good timber going to rot."

"Where're you going to now, Tattie Bogle?" Rannie wanted to know.

"To get peats."

"Pete's what? Oh *peats*. Where about?"

Gardner patted Desmond's neck while the little garron cropped gratefully at the grass. "No peats round here, Jack. You'll need to go much further out. I could show you where, if you like."

"That's what I was hoping. D'you know how to dig for the stuff? I've got this funny looking spade, see?"

He picked out of the cart the long-bladed implement with its long shaft, a spade especially designed for digging out slabs of peat. "This thing was in Flo Jinty's stick shed. She says peats are great burning fuel in the winter-time, so I thought I'd have a go at it. I'd not turn down some help, of course."

"Aye, well, seeing you helped with the logs . . ." Gardner murmured. "Come on, then. Best make back for the Pony Road. It goes straight out to some old peat bogs. Probably why the Pony Road's there, actually."

Betsy had a misgiving. "That'll be too near the Haggs. D'you think? Rannie . . ." Her voice tailed off. Rannie and ready-made danger, in her view, shouldn't be brought together. She had a heart-stopping vision of her brother trying to leap over one of the dreaded patches and failing to make it.

"You're no leaving *me*!" Rannie protested. "I want to go with Tattie Bogle. I'll sit in the cartie and stack the peat, or lead Desmond for him. Even carry the jam bag for Betsy. Honest!"

"Well . . . as long as you keep near the rest of us. None of your stravaiging away," Gardner warned. He turned to Jack. "You'll no be able to bring in any right off. It has to be stacked up like so," he said, leaning his hands sideways against each other," until it's dried out. *Then* you can gather it in and bring it home."

"Right. Anyway, it'll be good for young Des here to come out and get him used to carting. Hi-yup, lad! Want to get in, Nan?"

Nan was lifted into the cart, its first passenger. Her head was barely visible above its high sides.

Jack laughed. "Here, sit on my jersey."

Soon, having reached the Pony Road, the cart moved more easily, and now the expedition made progress towards the peat field that Gardner knew well from his many skirtings of it with their father on many a morning's gathering of the flocks. He led them confidently on for a good mile before stopping to take fresh bearing.

"It should be just over this wee bit rise ahead. Now — when we get to the edge of the peat moss, it's quite safe, but no wandering off, any of you. Mind! If I dare go home minus a Blair I'll get my head in my hands to play with." But his jocularity was still serious, and they knew it. "I suppose we shouldn't even be doing this on our own. Peat is tough to get out."

"Well, we'll see," said Jack, who had long practice in doing a great deal on his own — meaning without adults to supervise or help.

"Anyway, we can make a start. Only just, mind. Jocky gets hungry faster than us, and then it's a bee-line for home. Eh, Jocky?"

Jocky looked anxious for a moment at the thought of being suddenly hungry and far from food. He was the one who got shaky at the knees from hunger and that was a desperate situation because then his famous speediness of foot was drastically cut down just when he most needed it.

"Never mind," Gardner assured him, "we're no that desperate far away."

Taking Jack's special spade, he set to work breaking into the side of one of the dark banks scattered about. He dug away several spadefuls of the dry surface layer before reaching his first proper slab of peat. "There. That's just to show you what it looks like."

"It looks," Jack said, "like that stuff you eat."

"Fudge?"

"Yes. All bendy and shiny."

"I'll try here now."

Gardner chose a natural break in the terrain to begin his trench. It was hard work and a bit boring to watch. Betsy leaned against the cart with her elbows, gazing off across the hill. Some way in front of them was the start of the Haggs, she supposed. Gardner had said that this wasn't the main set of them, however. Only a couple were here, he'd said. She let her eye wander to the far horizon. Over yonder, she thought, was where that Mallard Loch was. There was supposed to be a sort of track out to it from the Back of the World, a rough trail only passable by horse and cart or Landrover, for the convenience of fishers who paid Sir Guy for the fishing of the loch.

The Mallard Loch ewes were scattered about their heft, recently calmed from the lamb weaning which left them unsettled for a couple of days. They certainly looked peaceful enough, drifting as they grazed.

Out here, the mountains of Argyll, always present in the distance in any view from Mowdy Mains, looked nearer. Betsy wondered if Argyll might be their next place to live. At least, if they moved to some spot near yon mountain, the one that looked to her like a helmet, she'd climb to its summit some day and look back across the Firth to this dear part of the world.

"Why's yon sheep running like that, Betsy?" Nan's voice broke into her thoughts.

"What sheep? Where? Oh, I see. Flies probably.

They sometimes have a wee mad run to themselves to get away from them."

She began to turn away to see how Gardner and the boys were getting on when something made her stop and sharpen her look.

"Gardner! Something's bothering the sheep. Look."

He straightened up. "Blast! No again."

As they watched, unable to do anything else, they could see two ewes fleeing in awkward haste from their would-be attacker, unmistakeably a large dog. The sheep did some desperate zig-zagging in their efforts to escape. One managed to get away, but only because the dog decided to concentrate on the other one. This poor victim came streaking and swerving across the hill straight to where the Blairs and Jack were standing. She began leaping as she came, instinctively clearing the patches of bog in her path. But her terrified energy was waning and with it her sense of safe ground. Her pursuer, equally blind to danger in his urge to kill, joined her in her last panicked leap. They landed together, his fangs fast in her throat, right in the middle of the ominous, weed-green pool.

Their composite weight and struggle caused the sinking to begin at once. The frightful crime and punishment was accomplished simultaneously before an awestruck audience. Then the hill was quiet and peaceful again, except for the drone of some engine far away, carried on the air across the empty expanse.

"It was an Alsatian, wasn't it?" whispered Betsy. She pulled her gaze away from the horrible pool which still seemed to be twitching about, as though rearranging itself to receive its burden deeper into itself. She turned to ask Gardner if he'd been able to make out anything special in the dog's markings and found him peering through his fieldglasses in the direction of Mallard Loch. He moved them along the skyline steadily, then stopped, went back, then found a focus.

"What've you seen?" she asked.

He handed her the powerful, ex-army fieldglasses. "See what you think."

She looked carefully. "It's a Landrover, no very big. Seems to be leaving the loch, maybe. You have a look, Jack."

Jack looked, Rannie looked, Jocky had a go, and even Nan could see the small vehicle moving along the horizon.

"Whoever they are," said Gardner grimly, "I'm positive that brute was with them."

"I've seen that Landrover before," said Jocky.

"What d'you mean? There's thousands like that." Rannie was scornful.

"Wait a minute. How d'you know you've seen it before?" Jack asked.

"That's what I don't know. I just had a feeling I had."

They were all quiet for a few moments, subdued by the death in the hagg and by the recurrence of what looked like deliberate devilment in their lives again. With no heart for further peat-digging now, they set off for home. They parted company with

Jack and Desmond, giving him the jam to give to Flo Jinty. They'd see him soon.

Jocky had been silent and thoughtful all the way home. All at once he stopped. "I mind now where I saw it!" he cried. "On Fergie Drummond's desk!"

"*What?*"

"Lena's wee brother?"

"How d'you mean, on his *desk*?"

He repeated his discovery. "Just what I said. It was a painting he did in Art. He's nuts about motors and never draws anything else. He did this green Landrover with that same silver wiggle all along its side. He said it stood for a name."

"*What* name?"

Jocky walked along slowly, trying to remember, muttering. "Silver something . . . silver river — no — silver *burn*? That's it! *Silverburn.*"

"So where did Fergie see a vehicle like that, then?"

"Don't know. Must've been in the village or in the Square at the Howe where he lives."

Betsy's mind immediately flew to Ty Weaver, the grieve at the Howe, who already meant something worrisome to her. *Silverburn* sounded like such a nice name, but from the look of things it might have something hagg-like underneath. The incident out by the Haggs smacked of something like natural justice. She hoped that more things would right themselves, if they just waited.

11

Something for Nosey Folk

It was very common for the Blairs and other children to be told by adults, "Ask no questions and you'll be told no lies." Even among themselves, children were used to giving the mildest of questions the smart retort "Nothing for nosey folk!" Even if you came to your own amiable mother to ask what was for the tea today, she might very easily tell you, "A run round the table and a kick at the cat!" Consequently, the best way to satisfy curiosity about anything was simply to watch, listen, and sniff — like nature's best nosey folk.

A lot could be picked up, however, when folk were terribly busy with important events and occasions, when folk gathered and gossiped, when children were seen and not heard much.

Such was the occasion of the Harvest Home early that October, held at the Howe as it had been for years. To mark the end of a successful harvest, funded by Sir Guy and organised by the folk who lived round the Square, including Lena Drummond's mother, the barn dance took place in the long, raftered hayloft above some stone sheds that housed the tractor and other farm vehicles. All the families of the estate came, but it was thought desirable to sell some tickets to "outsiders" too in order to achieve a "good mix".

Everybody helped, but the most important job by far was performed by the children. This was to "do the floor". No Harvest Home dance could be expected to go with a swing without a good floor. It was as important as the band and the dancers themselves. Many a poor dance was accredited to its "awfy bad flair" and a splendid one to its "braw flair". A braw flair, then, had to be slippery and smooth. To achieve this, as many children as possible were invited to come the day before. They were handed a tin of French chalk which they'd strew on the boards. Then they'd slide about in old slippers at first, then in their socks, building up a polish necessary for waltzes, fox-trots, strathspeys and Dashing White Sergeants. The floor at the Howe had always had a good reputation with dancers in the countryside and every year folk looked forward to the Harvest Home there.

This particular year, the floor was becoming especially good because of certain inspired variations on the sliding about that came from the combination of the Blairs, Jack, Look Slippy, the Drummond bairns, some old horse blankets, a couple of wide, padded brushes, and several straw-filled sacks tied at the neck with binder-twine. Gentle, solitary sliding developed into combinations of tricky moves in the air before landing on a blanket and finishing with a fast glide. Races with the brushes involved pushing a partner along the floor on a blanket at speed. The sacks were used much like sledges, with an initial running push and then a throwing on of the body to see how far the momentum would take you. Occasionally, someone would remember what they were doing all this for and they'd have a test of the surface. While Lena stylishly rendered "Come o'er the stream, Chairlie", the others tried to waltz the way they'd seen the big folk do it. But the floor always needed more work on it, and they'd return to what they did better.

At one point, tired with the exertion and thirsty, Betsy said to Gardner, "I'm away to Mrs Drummond's for a drink."

"I'll come as well. Maybe get a couple of bottles of water for the rest. No use trekking into her house one after the other."

"Right! We're away for water," she called to Lena. "Watch Nan for me."

They went down the stairs leading from the loft into the steading. At the bottom they both stopped short. In the steading stood a small Landrover with an undulating silver band painted along its side. They spoke together.

"Jocky's Landrover."

"Fergie's Landrover."

At that moment, from the far entrance to the steading came two men talking together. One was Weaver the Grieve and the other was a tall, very sun-tanned man wearing light-coloured clothes, including an almost white peaked cap. Betsy and Gardner stole softly past the Landrover on one side as the two men came up on the other and the man opened the driver's door. Weaver the Grieve saw them, but absently, and paid them no heed.

"Right, Ty," the other man was saying. "Things should be all set by November. You'll let me know, then?"

"I will that, Mr Silverburn," they heard Ty Weaver reply.

They looked at each other. "Silverburn, eh?" Gardner muttered. "I wonder who *he* is when he's at home. Looks kind of foreign, maybe."

"Yes, I wonder what he meant about November. That's the term time, when we're supposed to be flitting, though it hasn't been mentioned lately."

They passed the door of the house where the Weavers lived. No children lived in that house. Lena Drummond's mother had been heard to say "that's what's wrong", but she was always darkly hinting at things which Lena usually passed on with significant looks that nobody got.

Betsy went to knock on the Drummonds' door which was standing ajar, but she hesitated at the sound of voices inside the kitchen beyond the door. Lena Drummond's mother had a clear carrying voice which she had to have to communicate with Airchie Drummond, the dairyman, her husband, who'd been somewhat deaf on one side since the day someone threw a cabbage at his head "for fun". They listened.

"Well," Mrs Drummond was saying, "I suppose there's more money to be made in the caravan caper, but the farm just won't be the same. And what about the workers?"

"The grieve says they'll only be getting rid of half the herd, just enough to have milk for the caravan folk and feed the calves they'll be fattening for the market. Anyway, I don't see myself taking to that Silverburn. He should've stayed in South Africa where he belongs."

"Aye, well, he made a mint *there*, of course. Now he wants to spend it, buying up folks' places and turning them into God knows what. So. Have you made up your mind to go with Sir Guy, then? And what about the grieve? Is he for staying on here?"

"Oh, aye. I'll go with Sir Guy to his new place, that's if he's offering jobs there. He'll be needing some experienced men about."

There was a pause. Betsy again made to knock, but the next question stopped her.

"What about the Blairs? Are they safe enough? And the other farms?"

Airchie's boots could be heard shifting position on the kitchen floor. He gave a kind of dubious laugh. "I hear Black Hill and Ballin Farm are to be kept and the tenancy offered to Matt and Geordie. They've wanted that for years. It's a fine arrangement for everybody. I wouldn't say the same for Mowdy Mains, though. This Silverburn talks about taking it over as well, getting rid of the sheep, foresting the whole hill with big government grants, and turning the steading into a holiday place."

Betsy's hand cupped her mouth in dismay. Gardner looked at the ground and made to turn away from such dismal tidings.

"That's a pity," Mrs Drummond went on. "Why can Ewan Blair no have the chance of his own tenancy like the rest? He'd make a good go of it. Why's Sir Guy prepared to let *that* place go? He could get a decent return from it and still leave Ewan his living. They like it up there, away from everywhere, and Ewan's a good shepherd, now isn't he?"

"One of the best. I don't suppose the Blairs have the money to take on a tenancy, anyway, and Sir Guy's been told by his accountant that Mowdy Mains is losing money, no paying for itself, like. I mean, if he's no able to keep on the Castle where his family's been for generations, he'll no be worrying about keeping on some wee failing farm away in the wilds."

"*Failing*, you say? I can hardly credit *that*. Did they no get top prices for their wool this year? And what about that lamb sale a fortnight ago? Did you no hear Mowdy Mains lambs got top prices again? If that's failing, what does he have to do to be a howling success?"

"Aye, well, it's all checks and balances, sort of thing. Accountancy, like. And the accountants say the Mowdy Mains forecast isn't desperate good. So there y'are."

Through the sound of running water at the sink,

Mrs Drummond's voice came clearly to the two eavesdroppers outside. "Airchie. D'you mind that first time that Silverburn man came to the Howe? He'd another chap with him yon time. At the time I thought he was someone from the Castle. D'you mind?"

"Aye. Green corduroy suit and kind of nervous looking. That was Sir Guy's accountant come to see the grieve, I suppose."

"What for?"

"Don't ask *me*. It's nothing to do with me." But all the same Airchie's voice sounded troubled. His wife wasn't fooled.

"Maybe no. But you think the same as me. He looked very pally with Silverburn."

"And why no? Seeing the man is Silverburn's accountant as well. So I hear, anyway."

"Oh, aye?" Mrs Drummond's tone was the one she used for conveying her famous dark hints. As though she'd given herself the chills by it, she muttered, "That door! Aye being left open. What a draught!" The two outside heard her steps coming to shut it. Hurriedly, Betsy lifted her knuckles to chap.

"Och, it's you, is it, Betsy! How're you coming with that floor, then?"

"We . . ." Betsy's voice dried up, she was so parched and wrought up from overhearing the conversation.

"Could we have some water to drink, Mrs

Drummond?" Gardner said. "Save you being bothered if we take some back to the rest as well."

"Very good, I'll get you something. Hold on."

She kindly returned with three bottles filled, one with water and two with her own home-made lemon squash. "There y'are! Will we see you at the Harvest Home the morn's night?"

They nodded, thanking her. On their way back to the loft, Gardner said, "This Harvest Home is a pure make-a-fool-of. What's to celebrate? It's just an excuse to have a do. It could be held anywhere at all — in the village hall, in the school."

"But there's always been a Harvest Home at the Howe. Last year's was great."

"Ty Weaver was just new to the place then. He'd only been here five months. The man's no use, Dad says."

Suddenly, before they began to climb the stairs to the hayloft, Betsy had an urge to tell Gardner what *she* knew about Ty Weaver. She looked about the steading. There was no sign of *him*. All the same, she lowered her voice.

"Gardner, listen. Mum was telling me the other day about him. She used to know him when they were young, *really* young, when she was in service in Edinburgh. There was a dance she went to and he was there, with two other boys. They were mill-workers from a paper mill outside the town. He didn't like it at the mill and wanted to go in the Navy. He danced awfully well and Mum liked that about him. Anyway, he started coming to see her on her afternoon off, you see, but she found out from one of the other boys that he had a sweetheart in his village who also worked at the paper-mill. You see the picture. When she asked him about this, he'd just grin at her and talk about a girl in every port. So anyway, when Mum got another place to go to, out in the country where she met Dad helping his father with his field sheep, she was glad to forget about Tyrone Weaver. Seems he did go into the Navy for several years, too, and then he got married and for some reason tried his hand at farm work. When a grieve was needed here, he came."

Gardner had listened with his usual considering look at the ground. "Did he know we were next door when he took the job?"

"Mum says she's almost sure he took it *because* we were here."

Gardner nodded. "Have you noticed that Mrs Weaver?"

"Yes. She's hardly ever seen about, though."

"Aye. But have you *noticed*?"

"Hm. It's just the hair, really. She's nothing *like* Mum — though she's bonnie enough, I suppose."

"So. D'you think all this year's trouble has been coming from *him*?"

"I don't know. But I think Mum and Dad find him some sort of worry."

Gardner sat down on the bottom step. Unscrewing the top of one of the bottles, he took a drink and handed it to Betsy, saying "That business of the slaughtered sheep last Christmas'll have something to do with it, I bet."

"What d'you mean?" So Gardner had a piece of the puzzle too!

"The grieve came and told Dad that Sir Guy wanted a couple of sheep slaughtered for Christmas, for use at the Castle, with a bit to be given to Ty Weaver and some to be kept for us. He told Dad the proper permission had been got and for doing the job we would get some regular feeding for the hens and the cow. Turned out Sir Guy knew nothing about this at all and the meat went elsewhere. Then Weaver stopped the feeding arrangement when Dad faced him with the question. Dad can't complain to Sir Guy because Weaver says he'll deny he asked for the slaughter to be done and say it was all Dad's own doing. So the only way out is for us to leave."

"How d'you know about all this?"

"Dad told me when we were out gathering for the clipping once. He told me not to mention it to anybody."

"Why did he tell you?"

"Because I asked him straight outright why the grieve wasn't fit to help with the handlings, like he said."

"I see. Right enough, if you ask in the right way sometimes, they'll tell you the whole story — the way Mum did with me, too."

"Aye. But I don't think they know the whole

story. This stuff we heard the Drummonds talking about, for instance. About this accountant."

"I wonder . . . I wonder if Elenore knows anything, or Look Slippy. Seems to me we could ask them to find out a bit. I wonder why things have to be done in such secret ways — like why haven't Elenore and Look Slippy mentioned Sir Guy giving up the Castle? I suppose it means they don't know."

"Well, maybe if folk knew all along the line, there'd be protests and fuss and deals would never get made — especially rotten deals. Still, if the dealers are trying to avoid protests, that means they know there's something to protest *about*, I'm thinking."

"Yes. In other words, something isn't *fair*! In fact, like you said, downright wrong. I think we should find out. Be nosey, like."

"Better get up by with these bottles now."

Upstairs, they found that the athletics had flagged considerably, except for Nan being pulled round the floor very fast on a blanket, liking it, but pleading with her steed, "It's too fast! Stop! Luke, Luke, stop!"

When drinks had been shared, the children rested. Gardner looked round at everybody. Perhaps he'd been about to say something to their double friend, for he began, "Look Sl . . ." and stopped. Something had changed. All summer, when projects were in progress or the children were at least on the move, the twins had often been seen apart, spending quite long periods of time singly with various Blairs.

But, at rest, they'd always drifted back together. Now, in the hayloft at rest, they were still apart, and now it was even slightly possible to see who was who. Gardner took a bash at it. "Luke?" he addressed the one beside Rannie and got a lift of the chin in response. "Lippi?" He turned to the one at his own side and she returned his look questioningly. "Will you do us a favour, eh?"

"Sure," said Luke.

"What is it?" asked Lippi, pushing her blond hair back. In her ears she had little ear-rings that he hadn't seen before. Gardner hesitated.

"Eh . . . are you any good at being nosey?"

Rannie pulled Luke's nose with a laugh. Luke brushed him away, eyeing Gardner with interest. "How d'you mean?"

Gardner seemed to be having trouble. Rannie rushed in. "Come on, Gardner. Spit and speak plain."

Betsy thought she understood Gardner's constraint. Here they were, the twins, happily beginning to be two separate people as their life lost its anxiety and they were almost daily in contact with other very individual children, and here *he* was, about to spring on them the rumour about the Castle changes. It could very well make them rush back to the security of total twinhood, to Look Slippy, their distrusting personality. That would be a shame, all right.

"You mean," Lippi was saying, "you want us to

sleuth about? At the Castle maybe?" She looked over at her brother who nodded. "Well, we *have* been. Uncle Guy has been so sad-looking lately and Elenore so angry-sad, and we kept being told that curiosity killed the cat. So we sleuthed and eavesdropped. And now we know."

"Now we know," echoed Luke.

There was a silence in the loft broken by the leftover rustling of the last straw sack to be hurtled along the floor. Then clamour started.

"What is it you now know?"

"D'you not want to tell us?"

"Is somebody going to die?"

"Has somebody already died?"

"Bet you've to go away to boarding school!"

"Is it Janey?"

"Or the horses?"

"Be *quiet*, the lot of you, for a minute!" This was Jack. "Let them tell us." He turned to Luke. "Are you going to?"

Luke gazed at his sister. "You tell them, Lippi. She's really the one that eavesdropped."

Lippi slid into the middle of the encircling group, taking the floor. "Right." It was funny, but now that they'd got the habit of speaking separately for quite long bits of talk, you could hear the difference. Hers was much quicker, stronger speech, while Luke had a softer, drawly way of talking.

"We were going to bed one night. There's this passage we have to go along, past Uncle Guy's library. As we went past, I heard somebody speaking in there, two voices, both men, and strangers. I wondered what two strangers were doing in Uncle Guy's library and him not there. Luke said obviously they were waiting for him to come, then he went on to bed. But I went back to listen. I don't know why, except I thought they were talking *about* Uncle Guy."

"What made you think that?" Betsy asked.

"Well, I thought one of them said *This old castle's too much for him*, but it was after I was past the door that I realised that was what it sounded like and that's why I went back."

"And then what did you here?"

"One was saying *D'you reckon he'll buy it?* And the other said *He's got no choice. It's all in the books.* And the first one laughed and said *His sort never looks at the books. Wouldn't understand them if he did.* And the *other* one said *Just as well, eh?* Then Uncle Guy came along the passage and I scooted."

"What did they mean?" Jocky wanted to know. "Your Uncle Guy's library must be chock full of books. Isn't he a great reader? How could they say he never looks at them?"

"Well, Luke and me, that's what we thought too."

"And what's he supposed to be buying? Some wee-er castle somewhere?"

Lippi got to her feet and went to lean on the wall with hands behind her back to deliver her next piece of information.

"We went to Uncle Guy the next morning and do you know what he told us? He's leasing the Castle to some rich manufacturer for ninety-nine years and looking for some country house to buy in the district, somewhere where we can still have our horses. We don't know where it's to be yet. Elenore says she refuses to go far away from here and that's flat. Guess why!"

There was a general murmur about Heidie Ross. Lippi went on, "The thing that makes Uncle Guy so sad is that Mowdy Mains has to be sold, too, because it's not paying, they tell him. Elenore doesn't believe that."

They fell quiet again, thinking, absently watching dust motes in the sun ray from the skylight. Nan's voice came from behind Betsy.

"Our dad has a book. It's a wee green book where he keeps his sheep counts. He told me. He's always writing in it. Eh, Gardner?"

They all looked at her and then Jack exclaimed, "*That's* what is meant! Not *library* books, but *business* books."

"It sounds to me," Gardner murmured, "as if maybe your uncle's business books might not be right, then. Like maybe they've been . . . oh . . . tampered with. What's the word? *Cooked*. That's it. Them that knows how to keep books will know how to 'cook' them, no doubt."

Jack was frowning. "I suppose nobody would think about checking or questioning unless —"

"— unless something didn't fit," finished Gardner.

Betsy had an idea then. "It's mathematics, isn't it? Figures and such. Dick Baxter would understand that stuff. What if we could get hold of those books of Sir Guy's and compare with our Dad's wee green book. Dick would see if things were matching right."

"Easy said," Gardner replied. "They're probably kept in some safe."

Luke said, "We could get Elenore . . . to get Uncle Guy . . . to ask for a look at them or something, and then . . . Could you get your Dad's little book to *us*? Where's he keep it?"

Nan knew. "Behind the wallie dug on the mantlepiece."

"What's that? A wallie dug?"

"China dog ornament," explained Betsy quickly. "We couldn't keep it long, though. He'd miss it and . . ."

"Same for Uncle Guy's — even if we *could* get hold of his records. Wait a minute! I heard him telling Elenore this morning that the latest breakdowns for Mowdy Mains had arrived. Something like that. Could that be anything useful?"

"*Anything* about Mowdy Mains would," Betsy said.

Rannie had begun listening to the talk with impatience, as he always did when complications sounded beyond them. But now the prospect of intrigue, of a mission, caught his interest. "*I* know!" he cried. "We could do it while the Harvest Home's on the go the morn's night. Dick Baxter'll be coming with his mother and father."

"That's right," said Lena. "My mother and dad have asked them."

"So?" said Jack. "What do we do, Rannie? Name your brilliant plan, lad."

Rannie leaned forward eagerly, pointing back and forth to Luke and Lippi. "You two — get what you can. We get Dad's wee green book. Meet somewhere secret, in the dark, hereabouts in this steading. While the dance is on, we'll never be missed — and then we can compare. We can slip the secret *documents* back to their places before the morning comes. It'll be great!"

Everybody agreed it was brilliant, as a plan, at least. Before leaving the loft, its floor as polished with "use" as it would ever be, it was also agreed not to speak of this to anyone yet, except to brief Dick at school the next day that they had a secret "brain job" for him to do.

While walking up the cart road back to Mowdy Mains, the Blairs and Jack spoke together, not about the mission, but about the phenomenon of Luke and Lippi.

"They're amazing, that pair!"

"Not so much a *pair* any more, either."

"No. I wonder what made them change from a double to two singles."

"Mr Ross says confidence in yourself is the key to true singlehood."

"Where'd their confidence come from, then?"
"Being liked, maybe?"
"Being liked by a lot of folk in one place."
"Elenore says it's because of us lot."
"How'd you know? Did she tell *you*?"
"No. I picked it up once when she was talking to Mum. She said they *had* to split up to get round us all, sort of thing, to take us on. Could be, eh?"
"Maybe aye and maybe hooch aye."

That seemed to be the preferred conclusion, as though leaving the thing its mystery was the proper way to look at it, after all. Mysteries, thought Betsy, that were benevolent and creative, like this one, could be left alone. But the other sort, the destructive, malevolent ones, those had to be sorted out and exploded, for everybody's peace of mind — even if a wee band of scruffy, nosey bairns had to do it!

12
The Game's a Bogey!

It was a fine, fresh, moonlit night as the Blair family walked down the cart road to the Harvest Home. Beside them was Jack, leading Desmond, with Flo Jinty in an old armchair fitted into the cart. They were all clad in new rig-outs that their mother had been working on with the expert help of Flo Jinty who had knitted sleeveless Fair Isle pullovers for the boys and short, fleecy white boleros for the girls.

Jack was wearing his beloved kilt, the pleats new pressed, with a new claw-pin made from a grouse's foot. Flo Jinty wore a heather-purple frock and soft grey shawl. She had a piece of black-beaded net over her hair and lace mittens on her hands. There she sat in her armchair like some old princess on tour.

Elenore Stewart had brought from the castle one day two sets of enormous blue velvet curtains that were to be discarded and, as they were much too grand-looking even in their old age for any of the Mowdy Mains rooms, they had been put away in a box under the stairs to come in handy some time. And they had come in most handy for the Blairs' Harvest Home rig-outs — three pairs of long trousers and two gathered skirts. There had even been enough remnants to fashion matching ties for the boys, hair bands for the girls, and a specially requested pocket for Jocky. Nothing could have been smarter, their mother declared. As for herself, the gold-coloured dress her sister in Australia had sent her was the very dab, while their father's one best suit, used for shows, sales, or dog trials, would do very well.

Getting ready had been strange. Their father had been done first and kept coming to help each of them in turn, re-doing the boys' ties, brushing Nan's hair, wiping their shoes with the polishing cloth. Then he'd gone to lean against the lintel of the bedroom door where their mother was getting dressed.

"Don't watch me, Ewan," she'd said, sounding shy.

"See and put on your *iley oolay*, then!" he'd advised, using the family joke-name for the only cosmetic their mother ever wore. "If it's to be our last Harvest Home, we'll go in style."

Only a few people had already arrived when the Blairs' party climbed into the hayloft. Chairs from every house in the Square had been brought to line the walls. Other seating was provided by hay-bales covered with blankets. At the far end, a platform made from bales and planks had been fashioned and on this were ranged the musicians — an accordionist, a fiddler, a flautist, a tambour, and "him on the spoons". The loft rafters were decorated with bunches of corn and rushes, streamers and balloons. Lanterns hung at intervals at the wall end of the beams. In the lantern light the polished floor gleamed. Everything looked both festive and mysterious.

Under one of the lanterns, up by the band, a man was talking to the fiddler, his foot up on the edge of the platform, leaning stylishly on his knee. He had his back to the rest of the hall, but even his back view looked elegant, for he was dressed in a pale blue suit that seemed it might shine in the dark. He wore a straw hat with a blue band and blue ruffles could be seen at the one visible wrist. His shoes were white. Now he turned.

"Oh, Ewan," Betsy heard their mother's whispered cry. "Look at him!"

"Aye," was the reply. "Dressed to kill, as they say. In his element, isn't he!"

Ty Weaver strode down the polished floor towards them. Betsy couldn't take her eyes off him, he looked so fabulous, and he walked with such an attractive spring in his step. He swept off his hat and held it to his chest as he greeted the new-comers. "Isabel. Ewan. Miss Macrae. Isabel. Coats over there in the corner." Then he fixed his hat back on his head and disappeared down the stairs like a man on the run.

Looking at their parents, knowing what she knew, Betsy wondered painfully if it had been that good an idea to attend this evening. Their mother did look troubled, smoothing her hair nervously, shaking her head slightly at their father. He took her shoulder briefly and said, "There'll be no trouble. We'll see the night through, cool and canny. There's other folk to think of besides us, mind. Let the man enjoy his fine feathers. It's all he's got!"

Very soon, all the people came, including the Baxters, and the music began. Ty Weaver took his place on the platform with the band to welcome everybody and announce the dances one by one. He was such a far cry tonight from the previous, aimless, somewhat sleekit image Betsy had had of him that she followed his every movement with astonishment. Of course, right enough, whoever was the master of ceremonies had to be a bit of a showman to do the job well. All the same, this transformation was like a Frog Prince act, she thought. Such magical changes had to be the result of some special touch, some special presence, hadn't they?

After watching him for just a little while, noting the way he danced with his partners, his eyes scanning the other couples all the time, Betsy got infected with the expectancy in the man's bearing. She knew it was only a matter of time before he got his heart's desire, as dancers changed partners throughout the evening. All the men would follow the expected courtesy of taking other men's wives up on the floor at least once. Mrs Weaver hadn't come. She was said to be unwell.

Another person was watching the dazzling Ty as closely as Betsy. From her chair along the wall, her mittened hands clasped in her lap, Flo Jinty watched.

Elenore arrived with Luke and Lippi, with Mr Ross at her back. Sir Guy, it was learned, would make an appearance later on, to thank his people for a good harvest and drink their health. Luke was splendidly kilted, Lippi in a white dress with tartan sash.

"You're a' Hielan'," said Rannie in greeting. "What've you got in that wee sporran of yours? Give us a look!"

But Luke's warning glance and protective grab at his sporran was enough to tell the Blairs that his side of the mission had perhaps been fruitful.

Ty Weaver was announcing, "Now take your partners for an old-time waltz. Come on, everybody up! Bairns an' all."

The band began its medley with *Sweet Rothesay Bay*. Ewan Blair swung Wee Nan up into his arms and waltzed with her. Jack invited Betsy with a circular twirl of his finger in the air, Rannie took Lena, Jocky took Lippi, Gardner their mother, Luke Elenore, while Dick took his chance to quiz "him on the spoons" about his art, it not being required for this waltz. Flo Jinty watched and smiled under her net cap.

"And — change partners!" sang out someone as the tune changed to *Bonnie Gallowa'*. Without missing a beat, couples turned to the nearest other couple, changed partners and danced on. Young men desirous of capturing a certain partner could wait till they were within a beat of their goal and then sing out the cue for change. Watchful persons could then see who was after whom and exchange knowing looks.

"Watch this," whispered Betsy to Jack, as they drifted near Mr Ross and partner who in turn were drifting near Elenore and partner.

"Change partners!" called Mr Ross and Elenore together, waltzing smoothly into each other's arms and laughing at their ploy.

Gardner was standing alone, his partner swept away, the skirt of her lovely gold dress fluttering round the elegant blue trouser leg of her new partner as he circled them towards the edge of the floor where there was more room to move. More room was certainly needed, for they danced together with a wider, more sweeping, dipping grace than anyone there. It was noticed immediately. Gradually, people made more room until only two couples were left — Elenore and Mr Ross, Isa Blair and Ty Weaver. It was clearly a spectacle, as wonderful dancing always is, and people took to singing with the tune — *Helen of Kirkconnel* now — as they watched.

Standing with Gardner, Betsy watched their mother's face. It was perfectly grave, with what might have been concentration, her being on stage like this. Betsy thought it was more like strain. Ty Weaver's thin face was quite the opposite in its rapt expression, as though all the restfulness in the world lay with her he held in his arms. Across the floor, not singing, holding Nan on his knee, Ewan Blair, too, was a grave spectator.

Betsy could hardly stand the sight to go on any longer and willed a break to come. Nearby, Flo Jinty's clear blue eyes sparkled as she leaned forward in the lantern-shine, and suddenly Mr Ross seemed to collect himself, for he called out "Change partners!" just as the music built up to a close and applause rang among the rafters. Betsy turned to Flo Jinty again. The old "princess" was leaning back, satisfied. Betsy blinked and shook from her head a fleeting, ridiculous thought that had come into it. Her mind had been too much on daft story-book notions — Frog Prince, magic touch, old romantic music and such, when in fact she should be seeing to the business of the wee green book in Jocky's pocket and to whatever it was that Luke had hidden in his sporran. They should do something before refreshment time when folk would want to wander outside for a breath of air. Hide-and-seek round the steading in the dark at some point in the evening was considered a normal sideline for bairns at the Harvest Home, so there would be opportunity enough once *that* ploy was started.

But first there had to be some "turns" — songs or recitals from the floor by way of rest from dancing while still keeping up the entertainment, the children's contributions being especially enjoyed.

"Lena," Gardner was saying in a low voice, as the turns got underway now, beginning with *The Wee Inversneckie Store* from Rannie, followed by *The Farmer's Boy* from Mrs Drummond, "when you've done *your* turn, go and get your torches and we'll get the game going. They'll be raring to reel again soon and that'll be our chance. You be *het* first and draw out the game. Mind you don't look in the *wee* byre, for that's where Dick and me'll be."

Lena's turn, her favourite *If I were a Blackbird*, was next called for. Betsy remembered the last time she'd sung it, on the boat bound for Morlie Bay. Then it had been just a song, sad enough, but now it struck Betsy that its special longing strangely echoed something already in the air in the old loft.

The Dashing White Sergeant was being organised as the children crept downstairs into the steading, Nan holding onto Lippi's hand. By agreement, Jocky slipped to Dick from his velvet pocket the wee green book and Luke likewise handed over from his sporran a sheet of thin paper folded in half. Lena ran to her house to fetch two torches, one for the game and one to shed light on what they hoped might be crucial evidence.

The game had only run into its third *"het"*, which happened to be Betsy, when Gardner and Dick emerged from the wee byre. Dick's mathematical acumen had hardly been needed, as it turned out. The thing was so glaringly clear. The latest figures in the wee green book, purely private, to impress or trick no one, matched in no way those on the recent official record with its grand letterhead and seal.

"Come out, come out, wherever you are! The game's a bogey!" called Betsy, signifying that they were taking a break for a few moments' discussion. Huddled by the wee byre, they talked.

"Now we know something's fishy with the books."

"That's *their* game a bogey!"

"What'll we do?"

"Best put these back where they belong."

"Why?"

"We might be suspected of changing the figures in the wee book. They're only in pencil."

"What we have to do is just get Sir Guy to ask for a look at the wee book — out of the blue, like — and he'll see for himself."

"Yes, that's right. That's best." Luke was saying. He already had his sheet of paper in his hand. Suddenly, he grabbed from Gardner the wee green book as well and thrust it into his sporran, saying heartily, "Right, I'll copy it out and let you have it tomorrow. I'm useless at graphs."

Out of the tail of her eye, beyond the torchlight and their circle, Betsy saw what had made him pretend hurriedly that he was exchanging homework with one of them. The figure in the shining blue suit leaning on the corner of the byre had appeared out of the gloom. "I'm *het*!" shouted Rannie, grabbing the torch, and they scattered to their hiding places. From her place behind the tractor, Betsy saw Ty Weaver cross like a ghost to the stairs leading to the loft. She had no doubt that he had heard everything.

Yet he'd walked on by.

13

The High Danger Pipe

The Blairs were waiting at the appointed place the next day, expecting Luke and Lippi any moment. Off to the side of the Howe cart track ran a deep gulley, across which stretched at a height of some thirty feet a heavy iron water pipe running from the village reservoir to Mowdy Mains. It had never been a very good supply, and when an excellent spring had been discovered on the hill to become the family's drinking water, the old supply was discontinued. The old pipe, however, remained in place.

Some exciting balancing feats had been performed on it, from the usual cautious crossing, straddle-style, to a single heart-stopping run by Rannie once. At times of boredom, discontent or plain low spirits, a go across the High Danger Pipe was recommended. It was one of the few activities their parents did not know about.

At this moment, there was excitement enough waiting in the secluded gulley for the return of the wee green book.

The last part of the Harvest Home had been a confusion. Sir Guy had driven into the steading in the middle of the cover-up game and found Luke by the light of his headlights. "Luke?" They'd all heard his gruff bark of a voice. "Where's your sister?" Lippi had slid quickly to Luke's side and they'd been ushered back upstairs to the hayloft by their uncle. "Don't you know there's dangerous machinery in these sheds, and dangerous chemicals, no doubt? Not for children to play about in!"

They'd gone with him obediently. The others had followed, Jack muttering for them all, "He doesn't know half of the *real* danger."

While refreshments were taken by the gathering, Sir Guy had said his annual piece, full of thanks and blessings as usual. But at the end he had added an assurance that, though he himself would shortly be moving residence, he would continue to take a personal interest in this community which, he knew, would inevitably undergo some changes. He hoped these would not be too distressing, although he himself would rather have had it otherwise. As everyone probably had heard, the Howe and other bits of the estate were being considered for sale and excellent offers had been made by businessmen far richer than himself who would be able to put into the place what he could no longer afford. He hoped that the traditions of the community, like the Harvest Home, would be respected and upheld by whoever took over. He himself — and here he became especially gruff and barky, with a severe frown on his cast-down old face — felt deep chagrin that he'd failed to keep intact his inheritance, but forces beyond him . . . He'd glared at Luke who happened to be in his view as he looked up. Luke had grinned at him, out of sheer secret knowledge of a solution. His uncle had relaxed, given one more blessing, accepted the applause and a drink, mingled briefly with those gathered, and then left, taking Luke and Lippi with him. It had been nearly midnight.

The Drummonds had offered to let the Blair children and Jack go to sleep in their house if they got tired while the festivities went on till the wee hours, but there had been no need. First of all, Betsy had seen how Ty Weaver watched Luke very carefully till the boy left, still with the wee green book in his sporran. Luke had managed to whisper to them as he left, "Tomorrow morning — meet you by the pipe with it." With Luke gone, the grieve had seemed to drop his unpleasant vigilance and, as earlier in the evening, become that other cavalier creature that worried Betsy even more — and not just Betsy.

Twice more, their mother's by-gone beau had claimed her for dances that he himself had furtively requested from the band and then announced. Twice more, the picture they made together, her in her fluttery gold dress, him in his glamorous blue suit, had been striking — a romance of a picture. *He'd* known it, sought it and gloried in it. *She*, Betsy knew, had found it unpleasant but hadn't wanted to make any overt fuss by refusing to go up on the floor with someone whose invitation was courtesy itself.

"Why doesn't she just say no?" Gardner had said in an aside.

"Because she's not wanting to draw attention. She's trying to be casual, I suppose," Betsy had explained, though not at all sure she was right.

The last straw had been an "excuse me" dance. Their parents had been dancing together. Ty Weaver had tapped their father's shoulder to take over the dance. Airchie Drummond had tapped his. Then had come Mr Ross. Back had come their father, and again Ty Weaver had cut in. It had been a long dance, and each time their parents had got back together in it, there Ty Weaver had been, coming between them.

Their parents' conduct had kept the matter decorous, but it seemed that as the night wore on, the grieve had gradually lost any sense of his position of semi-host to this occasion. Perhaps he'd become a bit drunk and therefore uncaring? Had he been allowed to push his attentions further, there might have been some real alarm. As it was, however, the Blairs had left soon, pleading the tiredness of Flo Jinty and the bairns.

As they put on their coats to leave and descend the stairs, their father carrying a drooping Wee Nan, Ty Weaver had come at the last moment and taken their mother's hand. It was not like a handshake of goodbye, but a lifting of her fingertips, like the preliminary to an old-fashioned hand kiss. She'd quickly snatched her hand away, and Betsy had heard her saying, near to tears, "No more o' this, Ty. Grown man that you are, you've no sense."

His retort had been as quick as his dancing feet and as cavalier. "And who took it, eh?" He'd turned away, back to the noisy dancing, with one of those small puffs of weak laughter that can sound so like someone beginning to cry.

On the dark road home, Flo Jinty had held the sleeping Nan on her lap in her cart chair. The walk had been silent, all of them nearly asleep on their feet. At the Pony Road junction, Flo Jinty had said something to their mother as their two heads touched while transferring Nan from the cart. Betsy, who was nearest, had heard it clearly. "Now, do not go troubling yourself, Issabel, about yon divil. I haf had a word with him. Yess. One of my words."

Their mother had responded absently with, "I wouldn't waste my time," but Flo Jinty's words had lingered with Betsy long after.

Now, waiting by the High Danger Pipe, she thought of them again. She doubted that one of Flo Jinty's words would have any effect on someone with such a malicious will to harassment. He seemed to want both to harass *and* impress with his dreadful gaiety of the night before the same person — their mother. He'd apparently chosen this way of going about things, for reasons of his own (more like *un*reasons, really). What with all the harm he might have done already, Betsy was thinking, conspiring with other "divils" in the matter of the sheep worrying and the dog stealing, he was probably in too deep to back out and try to be a "nice fellie". It would be like going across the High Danger Pipe too far, getting fearfully stuck, the way back impossible, and nothing left to do but go on to the other side and hope you wouldn't fall off. They'd done it dozens of times for panic-fun.

Betsy had a swift image of Ty Weaver in his beautiful suit teetering on the highest part of the pipe, with Flo Jinty sitting on the grassy bank clasping her lace-mittened hands together, leaning forward intently as Betsy had seen her do last night at one point, having one of her words with him. Startled at her queer turn of mind, Betsy shook herself out of her daydream in time to see Luke, alone, riding up the road on Carlos. He waved.

As Luke joined them in the gulley under the High Danger Pipe, a tall figure appeared at the top of the far bank and looked down at them. His sheepskin waistcoat identified him. He began to hurry down the slope towards the little flock they made.

"It's the grieve."

"In an awful hurry, surely."

"He's after the wee green book, I bet," Betsy gasped. "He heard us last night. I *knew* he did."

"Give it to *me!*" Rannie offered cheerfully. "He'll never get it from *me.*"

With that, Rannie took the wee green book from Luke who was bending down to pass it to Gardner. Quick as a hare, he'd leaped across the burn and up the opposite bank. Perhaps thinking that Rannie was about to run home with the all-important notebook, Ty Weaver crossed the burn lower down and made to head Rannie off.

However, he misjudged. Stuffing the notebook into his back pocket, Rannie turned at the top of the bank and waited till Ty Weaver was almost within reach. Then, while the others watched in alarm, their brother sprang onto the concrete block nearby and began to cross to the middle of the High Danger Pipe.

The man either had the wits not to try to follow and risk startling the boy into a serious fall or he had himself a dread of heights. At any rate, his reaction was one of defeat. He stood with his hands on his hips and tried no more. He seemed to shrug as he dropped his arms and turned to look in the direction of Mowdy Mains. He looked long. Then, with a vague waving-away motion of his arm, as though to say "To the devil with it", and with no mind to those watching him, he set off down the track towards the Howe. His gait was kind of loose and staggering, like the Blairs' sometimes when they returned from their stravaigings, their legs folding with hunger, on the brink of collapsing.

Rannie returned cautiously to the safety of the bank.

"Good thinking," Luke commended. "What if you'd slipped!"

"Damn the fears!" Rannie answered. "I've never slipped off it yet."

Betsy rolled her eyes in relief at Jocky who had, like her, been expecting to race for help any moment.

"Anyway," Luke went on, turning Carlos' head to the cart road, "you'd better get your father's notebook put back before my Uncle Guy comes up. We talked to Elenore and she's got him convinced that he needs to look at his papers personally now and speak to your father himself. I'm off! See you later."

The problem now was how to get the notebook put back as quickly as possible without being seen at it. "We're lucky he hasn't missed it already," said Gardner wryly. "Come on. Think of some diversion, somebody. I mean, if Dad's in the living-room right now, he's bound to see . . ."

"Easy," said Rannie. "Here!" He handed the notebook to Betsy and again he jumped onto the High Danger Pipe. This time he made a great show of jelly legs all the way to the middle where his apparent faint heart got the better of him and he froze. Slowly, he bent his knees and lay along the pipe, clasping it with his arms and legs.

"I'm stuck!" he cried. "Can't move! Lost my nerve! *Get Dad!*"

The others allowed themselves a short splutter of conspiratorial laughter. Then they made for the house at top speed.

They weren't a minute too soon. Rushing indoors, they were in time to see their father searching through the envelopes and papers accumulated behind the wallie dug on the mantlepiece. He had a puzzled frown on his face.

"Quick, Dad! It's Rannie. He's got stuck on the big pipe across the gulley."

Their father stood stock still for a moment, taking in their words. Then he was out the door and running across the field. Knowing that Rannie's nerve would be back by the time their father reached him, and having replaced the notebook where it belonged, the others sank on to the couch with relief.

"That'll be the end of the High Danger Pipe for us!" said Jocky. "Better be worth it, that's all."

14

The Sad Baddie

It was into November. Gales were sweeping across the hills that week from the Atlantic, and the Firth looked brimming full, grey and white-flecked. Thoughts of ships at sea in such weather brought back to mind John Livingstone on Skellen Isle and how different things had been at Mowdy Mains when Betsy and Gardner had last seen him. Now they were able to send him better news of their circumstances and could attempt some explanation, as they understood it, for the devilment he'd spoken of when Young Laird had so mysteriously crawled ashore on his island.

Dear John (ran Betsy's part of the letter),
 I hope your lighthouse doesn't get blown down in this gale and that the *Bird on the Wing* is all right in her cave on her hooks.
 Young Laird is fine and working very well. Matt Fleming (at the farm neighbouring ours) has a nice collie called Gyp that's had pups by Young Laird. I've asked our Dad if the one that looks like Laird could go to you and he said he'd see.
 You were right about the devilment. Some man called Silverburn was planning to buy big

bits of our laird's estate for his business (caravans and holiday homes) and some of his so-called "contacts", including the grieve here, thought they'd have a better future with him and his plans. It's quite complicated and fishy because it seems *he* denies putting them up to shenanigans while they say he *did* — not in straight words but by digs and hints about back-handers and such. He says he had nothing to do with the men who stole Young Laird and took him out to sea in his boat, the same ones who "borrowed" Dick Baxter's uncle's Alsatian beast and set it on our sheep several times. He says he can't be blamed for over keenness in his supporters, and he refused to pay a penny for the worried sheep.

Anyway, the laird came up to see our Dad and they compared notes. The laird said he should have done it long ago. He turned down Silverburn's offer to buy the Howe *and* Mowdy Mains and brought in a new accountant to look into his affairs. The other one had been one of Silverburn's famous contacts and had stewed the books something terrible. The laird is keeping the two farms, now that he's been shown that they don't lose him money. The idea, as you can see, had been to harass us into leaving and to diddle the laird. The grieve is leaving soon, no doubt to run some Silverburn caravan site somewhere, and my friend Lena's Dad is to take over. The grieve's wife, always a very close woman, according to

Lena's mother, has already gone away, nobody knows where. The laird is moving from the Castle because it's too big and costs the earth to heat, but we hear he won't be going far. I hope not, because there are two bairns who live with him that I'd like to bring to Morlie Bay sometime — before we all grow up and have to start chasing our destiny.
Over to my brother. Goodbye from me,
Betsy Blair

Betsy wasn't sure about that last bit. It made her imagine something getting away from you, like chasing a rainbow or a hare, something uncatchable, when surely destiny was something that happened to you, that caught *you*, that was *meant* for you, no matter how you jooked about. Good or bad, it got you in the end. She sucked the end of her pencil, musing by the window in her room.

"What're you thinking about, Betsy?" It was Nan coming to stand beside her and look out at the gale.

"Oh, I was remembering that dog that went into the hagg with that sheep yon time."

"Why? It served the dog right."

"Yes, it did, quite right."

Nan drew on the steamy window pane. "Are bad things always served right?"

"Maybe not right away. But in the end, usually."

"Like the dog in the Haggs, the story of the Haggs," Wee Nan murmured to herself. "Poor sheep, though."

"Hm. The story of the Haggs is right," echoed Betsy softly, thinking of unpitying destiny catching up with rogues all over the world who'd been thinking they were getting away with something.

She took her letter downstairs for Gardner to add his bit on the back. He read through what she'd written first and added a few words of his own.

There's more to the grieve, John, than my sister has told you. You'll say he's well-named, for he has an old *grievance* against our Mother for not marrying him years ago when they were young. He must never have got over that and it has affected his nature. He's been trying to hurt our family in sleekit ways and playing along with Silverburn's plans. You should have seen him at the Harvest Home, too, all dressed up and acting all romantic with our Mother — just to vex her, I think. But he was vexing himself as well, because it's all up with him here. Our Mother and Dad seem to feel sorry for him now, but I'm not so sure they should.

I think you'll get a pup all right. Dad has said how much he's obliged to you for looking after Young Laird and when he says he'll see, that generally means he'll see *to it*.

Cheers!
Gardner Blair

Their mother could be heard in the kitchen slapping with the butter spades on the lid of the

churn and speaking between slaps. "You just —
(slap) — don't know what — (slap) — to get up to
— (slap) — next. Wind or no wind — (slap) — I
wish you'd — (slap) — go out and — (slap, slap) —
play!"

Gardner looked in the direction of the slaps.
"There's *somebody* getting laldie."

"Hm. Cooped up too long. Two whole days."

"Two whole hours is too long for that pair." He
got up and went to the sea-facing window. "Not
raining now. There's a break in the clouds." He
went through to the kitchen and soon Betsy heard
the back door slamming and the sound of running
feet as the boys raced away. Their mother came
through from the kitchen.

"Betsy, they're away to Ballin Glen. Nan wants to
go. Go on and take her."

Wrapped and buttoned against the wind, the girls
followed their brothers. It was a wild wind that blew,
sometimes pushing at their front, sometimes whirling
at their backs and shoving them forward so that they
could lean on it as they ran. They played with it,
laughing at the way it nudged and chased them about
the hill till they ducked down out of the worst of it into
the glen. They made for the *Bonnie Beech Bark*, at its
most exciting in flood-time and gale.

They could hear the hollow thundering of the
burn in spate, see through the trees the dark brown
torrent surging past carrying broken branches and
sods torn from the beleaguered banks.

Rannie came to a tottering stop, grasping Jocky, ahead of the others. "Hey! It's down. The *Beech Bark*. Foundered. Look at that!"

They looked in dismay, for it was true. Their wonderful ship, its anchored roots at last undermined by the flood, had keeled over entirely. Most of its top rigging was under water, a few unsubmerged branches trembling in the air as the tumbling water tugged at them.

"That's her finished, poor bark," lamented Jocky.

They approached slowly to inspect the drowned tree-ship.

"There's a sheep, Betsy. See? A poor drowned sheep caught in the branches under the water." Nan pointed.

"So it is. We've arrived too late to . . . save . . . this . . . one." Betsy's voice tailed off. She put out both arms to hold the boys behind her. "Wait!"

The patch of white fleece lifted among the top rigging. The water fell away slightly. She looked closer. The thing lifted, the water fell away, it lifted . . .

Betsy turned to Gardner swiftly, her thumb against her teeth. She knew it was no use trying to keep them all from seeing, but at least there wasn't all that much visible. "It's not a sheep, Gardner," she said in a low voice, staring at the water.

"Hey! That's no a sheep!" cried Rannie in a loud shout, starting forward.

"Rannie. Ranald! Be still." Gardner stopped his brother with a firm tug.

Then even Rannie had to fall silent as they looked at the body in the water and at each other. He spoke the words for them all presently.

"It's Ty Weaver, isn't it? He's been drowned."

"Aye," Gardner said. "It's the grieve all right. That's his waistcoat. He's caught in the branches under the water."

"Should we try and get him out?" Jocky asked anxiously.

"No use. We couldn't, anyway. Better get Dad and some of the men from the Howe. He's well caught. He'll no wash away."

They climbed out of the glen, hardly aware that the wind had dropped a good deal. As they reached the open hill, the sky above the Firth showed clear, with ragged, racing clouds over the far islands. Beyond them, Skellen Isle would be ringed by its white breakers. Betsy remembered the wind rising as their boat had crossed the sea to the island and how Lena had sung for the first time *If I were a Blackbird*. The longing words of it came into her mind now.

And in the top rigging I'd there build my nest,
And pillow my head on her lily-white breast.

He had been a baddie all right, but not always. And that was sad. Saddest of all was this. They all felt it.

15

Tokens of a Bonny Day

The November term had come and gone. The Blairs remained at Mowdy Mains, after all. Yet changes were still in the offing. Sir Guy had bought a fine Hall with small farm "over the hills somewhere in the next county", so that their likeable friends, Luke and Lippi, not to mention Carlos and Carmen, had already gone from their daily lives. Granted, when Betsy, Gardner, and Jack moved on soon from the village school to travel to Greenbeg High School by bus, they would likely be in the same school as Luke and Lippi. Rannie, too, within a couple of years would follow and meet up with Luke again. But it wasn't going to be quite the same as having them living just down the road.

Then, too, Mr Ross was said to be moving as well at the end of the year. He hadn't said anything to the Blairs, but Lena Drummond's mother knew. One morning in the classroom, Betsy found herself staring gloomily at their teacher, thinking about his greatness with all of them and finding a tiny bit of a jeery-sneer coming on to do with his greatness with Elenore Stewart which, no doubt, was the cause of his going to leave. She dared say he was probably going to follow his love.

The idea recalled Lena's blackbird song and Ty Weaver's sorry end, turning romance of that sort into a kind of poetic daftness that she didn't like to think Mr Ross would have any truck with. She didn't like the idea at all of love being a mysterious power that could change folks' courses like that and even shipwreck them. Folk needed to watch that, she decided, her frown deepening.

The class ended for playtime. As she passed Mr Ross's high desk on its platform, still glowering, he spoke. "Betsy, if you could see your face! Like somebody that's lost ten pence and found five. Things been too much for you lately?" He patted the edge of his desk by her face. "Here. Take a load off your shoulders."

She gave him a wry look and put her palms on the desk followed by her chin, a popular stance with pupils having a chat with Mr Ross. She decided to tell him exactly what bothered her. "It's you," she said.

"*Me?*"

"Aye, *you*. You never told us you were going away. Why not?"

"Well, Betsy — what a place this village is for nosey folk! But it's a good thing, too, in its own way. The thing is, I've not been sure, you see. I had to find out a few things. And now I have, I can tell you. I *will* be leaving the village by next June. That could be good news for some folk, you know. Not everybody agrees with my educational methods."

"It's bad news for us, anyway," Betsy grumbled. "Gardner and Jack say the same."

Mr Ross smiled. "But we'll all be moving from the school at the same time."

"Aye, but *you'll* no be going to Greenbeg High." Seeing him smile again, a thought struck her. "Will you? *Will you?* That'd be great!"

He laughed out loud. "Listen. I'm having a change, and that's it."

"Aye, you're going to go and marry Elenore, aren't you. Everybody knew that months ago."

"*Did* they now! Well, *I* didn't. It was one of the things I had to find out."

"You could still teach at Greenbeg High, though," she declared eagerly.

"I could, yes. But I want to be a learner now, not a teacher. Is that so bad?"

"How d'you mean, a learner? You're a good teacher, Mr Ross."

"Ah, but I might be a better learner."

"Anyway, who's going to teach *you*, then?"

"A very experienced man or two. They've already started, really."

"What're they going to teach you?"

"Their trade."

"What's that?"

He scratched his head drolly. "Sort of . . . farming."

She looked at him keenly. "Farming? With Elenore . . . Are you going to run Sir Guy's wee farm over by Greenbeg somewhere?"

"I hope so."

"You'll be living right beside Luke and Lippi, then."

"Yes. That's another thing I'm going to be learning, you see. Fathering."

"And who'll teach you *that*?" she asked ironically.

"Nobody ever teaches that exactly, more's the pity. But I can talk to other fathers – the same men who'll help me with farming — Ewan Blair, for one. And the bairns themselves will teach me. And Elenore, of course. I'll learn. I'm not worried about that."

She lifted her chin off the desk with a sigh. "That all sounds fine. We'll no see much of any of you, though, except when you make one of your *expeditions* back to Mowdy Mains for lessons."

Mr Ross laughed again, shaking his head as if he found her persistent gloom quite hilarious. Then he looked at her seriously and pointed his forefinger at her, saying, "Listen."

She listened and agreed to do as he said the next day, though she wasn't told exactly why.

The next morning, Saturday, the Blairs were up early, ready and curious about Mr Ross's instructions relayed by Betsy. They were to call on Jack first of all. It was a grey morning, cold and clear, but no wind to speak of.

Jack was splitting logs when they came into view.

They hailed him from the top of the glenside and, crossing the burn by a little footbridge that he'd made, they put to him their proposal.

"Let's go up yonder, Jack," Gardner said, pointing to the top of Ballin Brae, far beyond Flo Jinty's cottage where a stand of dark pines stood against the sky. "You've been up there, haven't you?"

Jack rested on his axe, squinting at them in the cold morning sun. He followed the direction of Gardner's pointing and gave a small smile. "Right," he agreed softly, "if you like. I've not been up there for ages myself. Sure, I'd like to go. There *is* something up there that you'll like."

"Been keeping it to yourself, eh?" Rannie accused. "What is it? Another treehouse of yours?"

"Well, no. Nothing *I've* made. It's a natural phenomenon. Help me stack these logs first."

He shouted in at the cottage door. "We're away up the hill. Right?" A muffled "Right you are" came from inside above the whirr of Flo Jinty's spinning wheel.

It was as well that Jack kept them in the dark about his natural phenomenon, for it was a long, climbing walk through deep heather and their curiosity kept them going. At one point Jack stopped to rest. The others tottered and fell around him. He looked at Gardner with special sympathy. "Carry Nan now? Next time she gives out? By the way, whose idea was this?"

Betsy answered, "Mr Ross's, actually. He says

he'll meet us up there. He's got something to show us as well. It's probably your natural phenomenon that he doesn't realise you've already discovered."

"Oh. I see. Probably so. On we go, then!"

The dense stand of Scots pines was getting nearer. Gradually, what seemed like total undergrowth blotting out the daylight between the trees proved to be something far more solid. What the trees were hiding, like sentinels drawn up in ranks to protect it, was an enormous outcropping of granite rock. Out of its crannies here and there were growing sprays of dead ferns, heather and faded grass, with grey-green patches of lichen everywhere. The face of it fronting them looked to be a sheer drop.

"Great for climbing on," Jack said, nudging Rannie whose face was alive with the very thought.

"Have you been up on it?" he breathed awestruck.

"Hm."

"How d'you go?"

For answer, Jack led them round the base of the rock to the right where they had to climb more of the hill. On this side the slope of the rock was gradual, falling away in steps that any child could manage. Without a word, silent with the marvel of it, they climbed on all fours to its crest. It was, though quite safe, terribly high. They had to rise carefully from their bent-over, climbing position to a shaky upright, so airy was it.

"Phew!"

"Great view!"

"There's a loch over there. I bet that's Mallard Loch."

"And yonder's the Back of the World."

"There's a town — Greenbeg, I think."

"Hey! There's chimneys and roofs below that ridge."

"Where?"

"There — down there, just before that glen road."

They turned and viewed, viewed and turned, the vistas were so splendid from up there on the rock. It was while they were turned facing the way they'd come, looking across the expanse of moorland that was Mowdy Mains ground, past it to the silver arm of the Firth, and farther still to the grey Argyll hills, that a faint hail was heard from behind. "Yoo hoo! Guess who!"

They turned round slowly, scanning the slopes below. "Who was that?"

"D'you see anybody, Nan?" they asked her with the brightest eyes of the lot. She pointed. "There! There they are!"

Now they saw, and were astonished. "We'll wait up here," Gardner said.

The newcomers approached, on foot, panting with the exertion of the climb from their side. The Blairs sat down on top of the rock to wait. Presently, from below, over the rim of the first ledge, appeared the two fair heads, and presently it was apparent that they were singing the well-known song of good cheer as they climbed.

Oh, we're no awa' tae bide awa',
Oh, we're no awa' tae leave ye,
Oh, we're no awa' tae bide awa',
We'll aye come back an' see ye.

To encourage them, the Blairs joined in the last two lines at the tops of their voices. It was the best way to express feelings of enthusiastic reunion, since anything more physical and boisterous would have been dodgy at that great height.

"Isn't this a terrific place!" Luke said, sitting on a flat bit. Lippi was ruffling Nan's hair in greeting.

"Where's Mr Ross, then? Betsy asked.

"Down at the Hall yonder." Luke nodded in the direction of the chimneys and tree-crowns far below.

"D'you miss the Castle?" she went on.

Luke patted the rock. "Not while we've got this. *This* is our castle."

"And ours," murmured Jack. "Folk need high places to come to. Sometimes . . . to be . . . you know." He spread wide his arms to indicate what he was trying to say and found the words just as the others were saying them for him.

"*Monarchs — of all they survey!*"